THE LOGIC OF RENEWAL

THE LOGIC OF RENEWAL

William J. Abraham

WILLIAM B. EERDMANS PUBLISHING COMPANY
GRAND RAPIDS, MICHIGAN / CAMBRIDGE, U.K.

© 2003 Wm. B. Eerdmans Publishing Co.

WM. B. EERDMANS PUBLISHING CO.
255 Jefferson Ave. S.E., Grand Rapids, Michigan 49503 /
P.O. Box 163, Cambridge CB3 9PU U.K.

Printed in the United States of America

08 07 06 05 04 03   7 6 5 4 3 2 1

Library of Congress Cataloging-in-Publication Data

Abraham, William J. (William James), 1947-
The logic of renewal / William J. Abraham.
p.   cm.
Includes bibliographical references and index.
ISBN 0-8028-2656-3 (pbk.: alk. paper)
1. Church renewal — History — 20th century.   I. Title.
BV600.3.A27   2003
262′.001′7 — dc22

2003049469

www.eerdmans.com

To Marselle Moore (1959-2000)

CONTENTS

Acknowledgments ix

1. The Logic of Renewal 1

2. Foundations and Food:
James T. Draper and Dennis Bennett 9

3. A Tale of Two Bishops:
Lesslie Newbigin and John Shelby Spong 25

4. Tensions in Rome:
Rosemary Radford Ruether and Cardinal Ratzinger 45

5. Dying for Renewal:
Martin Luther King Jr. and Archbishop Romero 71

6. Trojan Horses from Paris:
Alexander Schmemann and Gilbert Bilezikian 93

7. Postmodernity, or Death by One's Own Hand:
Don Cupitt and Edward Norman 111

8. Quaking in the Ruins:
C. Peter Wagner and R. R. Reno 133

9. Renewal and the Quest for Intellectual Integrity 153

ACKNOWLEDGMENTS

THIS BOOK HAS BENEFITED enormously from the response I received when I presented various parts of it as lectures in a number of places. Thus the early chapters were given as the thirteenth annual Carmichael-Walling Lectures at Abilene Christian University, The H. Orton Wiley Lectures at Point Loma Nazarene University, and The Warren Lectures at Dubuque University. I want to thank my wonderful hosts for their hospitality during these occasions.

Special thanks go to Canon Professor Andrew Walker for invigorating conversation and encouragement and to Jason Vickers for his splendid help in providing penetrating criticism and invaluable editing.

Some may wonder if there is any relationship between this and my earlier book on the logic of evangelism. There is. When I finished my work on evangelism, I was well aware that many local churches and denominations would find the practice of evangelism I have recommended to be challenging in the extreme. One can overcome this challenge by settling for lower standards in the practice of evangelism. There is a better route, however: to take the challenge of evangelism as a spur to radical renewal in the life of the church as a whole. Thus this book is a natural follow-up to my work on evangelism.

I have dedicated this book to Marselle Moore, who initially had an indirect but very significant hand in my coming to Perkins School of Theology, Southern Methodist University, a place of vigorous conversation and inquiry that has been my academic home for over seventeen years. Marselle was a very special friend who had many years ahead of him as a truly great leader in his church but who was tragically killed in a road accident. May his memory be eternal.

CHAPTER 1

THE LOGIC OF RENEWAL

THE WESTERN CHURCH IS currently awash in a sea of renewal movements. So much so that she is in danger of drowning. Across the denominations, even across the great theological divisions so prevalent in the contemporary church, there is a persistent quest for the kind of change that will enable the church to do the work of God in a healthy and forthright manner. We now have so much literature on the topic that one is hard pressed to keep up with it. The shape of the interest is reflected in the language deployed. We have developed over the years a whole family of concepts to capture what we might broadly refer to as renewal. Some speak of "revitalization," some of "reform," some of "awakening," some of "revival," and some of "restoration." Renewal is our contemporary jargon. It has effectively replaced the language of revival that has been so common in Protestant circles over the last three centuries.

For some, revival remains the paradigm of renewal. The great need of the hour, as they see it, is for another revival. The want to see a mighty outpouring of the Holy Spirit that will purge the church of her sin and fill her with Pentecostal fire so that the work of evangelism will be owned afresh as both joy and responsibility. I have some sympathy with this sentiment, in that I have enormous respect for what happened in and through revivals in the history of the Western church. Outside the West, revivals are by no means a spent force. However, as Albert Outler observed some years ago, we will not have a Third Great Awakening until we realize that the second one is over.[1]

Revivals, however, have been a thoroughly mixed affair, far from what the hagiography and myth-making have cracked them up to be. Jonathan Edwards, surely the acutest observer of revival that has ever lived, was right to spend a lot of time working on the pathology of revival.[2] John Wesley was a brilliant leader and an able thinker, yet the movement he reluctantly founded in the eighteenth century failed as a church to sustain its best insights and practices beyond a century and a half or so in North America. Charles Finney, surely one of the most interesting leaders of the nineteenth century, knew only too well that he had overly mechanized the means of revival and thus created space for all sorts of daft practices in the years to come.[3]

How are we construing renewal? Standard dictionaries give three different senses to this innocent little verb, "to renew." It can mean "to replace," as when we renew our driver's license after it has expired. It can also mean "to get again," "to make again," "to say again," or "to give again," as when we renew a lease, when we renew a subscription to a periodical, when we renew our attack, or when we renew our complaints. It can also mean to make as good as new, to put new life and vigor into, and to restore to the original condition. Clearly, it is the third sense that interests us here. We are interested in the recovery of the apostolic life and identity of the church, in the receiving of new life and vigor into the daily life of the church, both locally and nationally, and in the remaking of the church, so that she reflects her original, God-given intention and splendor.

From this broad definition, we can begin to sketch several considerations that are going to be relevant when we think through proposals about the renewal of the church.

---

1. I am working from memory at this point. Outler's incisive analysis is well worth reading and can be found in his "A Third Great Awakening?" in Albert C. Outler, *Evangelism and Theology in the Wesleyan Spirit* (Nashville: Discipleship Resources, 1996), pp. 41-55.

2. His two volumes on the awakenings of his day are extraordinarily perceptive. For his mature assessment see his *The Religious Affections*, ed. John E. Smith (New Haven: Yale University Press, 1959).

3. This is well brought out in his *Reflections on Revival* (Minneapolis: Bethany Fellowship, 1979).

1. Proposals in renewal will be inescapably theological in content. They will presuppose some sort of ecclesial picture of what the church is supposed to be and to do. It is all too easy to forget this, not least because Christians in the West are woefully weak in their thinking about ecclesiology. Either they refuse to think about it at all, or they simply accept uncritically the conception of the church that they have inherited. Yet ecclesiological considerations are crucial in any deep conception of ecclesial renewal. Our conceptions of renewal depend in part on some governing model of what the life and work of the church should be. We operate with some picture of how things really ought to be in the church at large.

2. Ignoring ecclesiological considerations in our thinking stems in large measure from casting of renewal in purely personal terms. Thus, following the Puritans and the Pietists, we tend to think of renewal as fundamentally the renewal of the individual. This leads naturally into the great Reformation themes of justification, regeneration, sanctification, grace, repentance, and the like. Richard F. Lovelace's fine book on renewal is a good example of this approach.[4] Insofar as we think of the church in this tradition, we think of the church as a collection of or voluntary association of suitably renewed or sanctified individuals. We need, however, to break loose from this sort of individualism and begin to think in terms of ecclesial as well as individual or personal renewal. To be sure, we cannot have ecclesial renewal without personal renewal, but there are deep dimensions of renewal that go well beyond what can be captured in discussion of personal or individual renewal. We shall attempt to focus on the corporate side of renewal in what follows.

3. Proposals about renewal invariably follow a simple pattern. They propose a description of the life of the church that depicts what is flawed in one way or another — we are told that the church is diseased or sick in some crucial respect. This leads to a diagnosis as to why the flaw or set of flaws has developed — we are given an account of the etiology of the sickness of the church. Finally, there is a prescription as to how to put

---

4. *The Dynamics of Spiritual Renewal: An Evangelical Theology of Renewal* (Downers Grove: InterVarsity Press, 1979).

things right — we are offered an account of the medicine that we need to take if the church is to be cured. This simple pattern is at the heart of virtually all conceptions of renewal. It constitutes the formal skeleton upon which the material proposals that follow are fleshed out and identified in detail.

4. Our extended use of the medical analogy prompts a fourth consideration. Renewal can go wrong in all sorts of ways. It can go wrong because of original misdescription, because of misdiagnosis, or because the doctor has prescribed the wrong medicine. In all these cases, the quest for renewal can be disastrous. It can all too easily lead to the killing of the patient. This is exactly what critics of renewal movements have noted. Perhaps the most celebrated criticism of all renewal movements in the history of the church can be found in Ronald Knox's massive study of "enthusiasm."[5] One suspects that Knox really had little time for the renewal movements of the seventeenth and eighteenth century, which he saw as doing more harm than good.

We need not go to the extremes of Knox in order to reckon with reality, but we must surely acknowledge the possibility of unintended side effects in proposals for renewal. Again and again, leading personalities or major movements have appeared who have identified some deep problem in the life of the church. They propose and implement a solution. The solution then takes on a life of its own, so that across the generations it has led to other equally serious problems. The two most conspicuous side effects of renewal are, in fact, judgmentalism and schism: those committed to renewal very quickly begin to see themselves as better than others, especially better than those others who do not share their vision of change, and they equally very quickly move to break up the body of Christ into factions and parties. Renewal then is often a paradoxical affair. It is a sobering thought to ponder that sometimes our best efforts wreak havoc in the body of Christ.

5. This leads naturally to a fifth point. Like it or not, there is no firm calculus for making good judgments in this arena. Perhaps this is why some people stay clear of the whole business of renewal. They are acutely

5. R. A. Knox, *Enthusiasm* (Oxford: Clarendon, 1950).

aware that, in thinking about renewal, what is ultimately needed is a very rich gift of ecclesial and spiritual discernment. It is easy to go astray; more specifically, it is easy to fall prey to a kind of spiritual utopianism. Karl Popper has made famous a distinction in politics between utopian social engineering and piecemeal social engineering. In the former case, the reformer opts for all sorts of revolutionary changes that are supposed to lead to the Promised Land. In the latter case, the reformer is more cautious, preferring to keep change within more manageable proportions. Popper is correct that the former is fraught with the perennial danger of totalitarianism; one can see this in the history of revival and renewal. On the one hand, people who crave for radical and substantial change often feel very incompetent and helpless. In such circumstances, they are liable to follow any leader who is confident enough to lead them to revival. On the other hand, there are leaders who are only all too keen to become spiritual dictators. They can easily develop spurious justifications for their fiscal and moral aberrations.

What this suggests is that there is no substitute for making good judgments in this arena. We can, of course, walk away and forget the whole matter. We can turn our backs on the topic of renewal and find something else to explore, but that would be an extreme reaction that, without any serious warrant, invites us to give up in despair. The better alternative is to muster all the good judgment and discernment we can muster and launch forth as best we can.

6. As a final point, and as a first exercise of that judgment, we should note that there is no necessity for renewal at all times in the history of the church. To put the matter bluntly, there are times when it is foolish and dangerous to call for ecclesial renewal.

We all know that some Christians very easily develop a kind of listless foot-and-mouth disease. They are always on the run to hear some new grand scheme for the renewal of the church. They run from this speaker to that speaker, from this conference to that conference, from this book to that book, from this set of tapes to that set of tapes, in search of the magic medicine that will cure the church of its various diseases. This is true of evangelism, too. We are all aware of the tendency to hearken to the flavor of the month. People run from Evangelism Explosion to church growth, from signs and wonders to exorcism and prophecy, from mega-movements in Korea to mega-churches in Chicago, searching enthusiastically for the principle or the program that will work for them.

There is something inherently incoherent about this kind of frenetic activity. It is theologically bizarre because renewal can only be a means to an end. Renewal is not itself the health of the church but a means to the restoration of health. Hence, at some point, the search has to stop. Most medicine should only be applied for a set period of time. Furthermore, there is only so much renewal a soul or a church can bear. To use a political analogy, permanent revolutions are destructive because they never know when to stop the reforming process. In the end people simply become exhausted, or the quest for renewal becomes a mechanism for achieving arbitrary power over others. This is the case in the long-standing desire of liberal Protestantism to renew the theological life of the church. Its leaders are now intellectually exhausted in their efforts to reform Christian doctrine to fit every new situation, and yet they are extremely reluctant to give up the academic and ecclesiastical power they gained in the twentieth century.

Another way to make this point is to say that the church needs a healthy sense of realism in its quest for renewal. Not every age or every time is a time for renewal. There are also seasons of consolidation, for example. Spiritual and theological gains must be properly institutionalized and stabilized. New insights have to be exploited and explored. New experiences need to be examined and evaluated. There are also times when the church has to hold on for dear life to its manifold treasures. Think, for example, of the current situation of the Orthodox church in Russia. A golden opportunity for renewal failed at the beginning of the twentieth century. Then everything went up in smoke as the Communists took over. For over seventy years the church did well merely to stay alive. To speak in those circumstances of renewal — that is, in those seventy years of brutal repression — is cruel and unrealistic, although one never wants to rule out the action of special providence to direct otherwise. It is well that the Russian Orthodox church managed to keep the faith alive across the generations, preserving its liturgical and canonical treasures for ages to come. Now that the oppressors have been overthrown, it is time to speak of renewal; earlier, such talk would have been premature, if not dangerous.

We might well ponder if this is to be our vocation in the West over the next generation or so. If philosophers like Alasdair MacIntyre[6] or cultural anthropologists like James Davison Hunter[7] are right, we had better get ready for a new dark age in our culture. Certainly, our culture faces some very stiff challenges. The collapse of Marxism has done nothing to mitigate the greed, the hedonism, the crass materialism, the ruthless competitive spirit, and the moral superficiality that are now the clear concomitants of democratic capitalism; if anything, they make things worse by creating a false and bogus sense of political superiority. The arrival of global terrorism will certainly not mitigate this latter possibility. It may well be, moreover, that the church in the West is so infected with the diseases of the very culture it has helped to create that not much can be expected from her as she enters a new century. In these circumstances, dreaming of the renewal of the church could well be a snare and a distraction. What may be needed, some might say, is a stoic sense of endurance and simple persistence. What is crucial, they might argue, is the ability to drag oneself across the desert sands that lie in wait for us up ahead.

I am certainly open to this kind of suggestion. In Ireland we even have a special verb to designate this kind of psychological strategy: we call it "tholing." People "thole" through a bad marriage; they "thole" through rough times at work; or they "thole" through the hard grind of preparations for medical exams. To "thole" means to put one's head down and simply survive from week to week. I am not then averse to reaching this conclusion. It should come, however, at the end rather than the beginning of our deliberations. At this stage in the debate, it is premature to say that MacIntyre and those in agreement with him are right in their analysis of Western civilization. The jury is still out. Moreover, even if MacIntyre is correct, we still need to give attention to the subject of renewal, for in so doing we may be able to get hold of matters that are essential to the very existence of the church in the postmodern world. In

6. Alasdair C. MacIntyre, *After Virtue* (Notre Dame: University of Notre Dame, 1981).

7. James Davison Hunter, *Culture Wars: The Struggle to Define America* (New York: Basic Books, 1991).

other words, even if all we can hope for is survival and the keeping alive of the faith for the grandchildren, we may best ensure such survival by thinking long and hard about the nature and dynamics of renewal. In our next chapter we shall proceed to pursue this line of inquiry by examining two very different conceptions of renewal that have surfaced within more conservative Christian circles in recent years.

Permit a final comment on how the book as a whole proceeds. The theological motor driving the work consists of a review of the most salient proposals on renewal that have surfaced over the last fifty years or so. Aside from the first and last chapters, I line up pairs of proposals that expose strongly contrasting convictions. I hope that readers will value the mapping that is involved, and that they will find themselves having a better understanding of the winds that are currently swirling around the church in the West. Simply getting our bearings is well worth the trouble of straightforward exposition and articulation of the alternatives on offer. There is one exception to this strategy. Right in the middle, in Chapter Five, for the sake of symmetry, I explore two proposals that are complementary. The reason for this departure is simple: the proposal at issue strikes me as exactly right and necessary for any healthy vision of the church for the future. In and around these expositions I shall begin to develop my own proposals about renewal by critical interaction with those under review. In the final chapter I shall come clean and lay out my positive proposals more formally. I understand the temptation to go straight to that chapter and find out where I am going, but it will be more interesting and illuminating to hold off and read the final chapter last.

FOUNDATIONS AND FOOD

JAMES T. DRAPER AND DENNIS BENNETT

MODERN FUNDAMENTALISTS AND charismatics often look back nostalgically on the revivals of the eighteenth and nineteenth century. In addition, they gravitate to a similar doctrine of Scripture. Beyond that they are deeply at odds with each other. Initially, it must appear odd to yoke together Fundamentalists and charismatics in the same chapter. Generally, they refuse to be in the same room together; some might even refuse to be seen dead together. In some situations they are sworn enemies, each seeing the other as the symptom of all that is wrong in the modern church. Yet, it is extremely useful to discuss them in tandem. Both represent movements that have enormous numbers behind them. Both take it as given that the way ahead lies not in one more modern revision of the Christian tradition but in the retrieval of historic Christian tradition. Both are in fact thoroughly conservative in that they insist on stoutly holding on to elements of the Christian tradition that have been at risk or jettisoned in the modern period.

In my exposition I shall draw on the irenic work of James T. Draper (1935-) to represent the Fundamentalists in the Southern Baptist Convention, and I shall draw on the landmark work of Dennis Bennett (1928-1991) to represent the charismatics. In both cases, I shall feel free to add in additional considerations that are prevalent in other exponents of both movements.

As we pick up the contribution of the Fundamentalists, it is important to acknowledge their stake in the debate. In my view, they deserve to be taken extremely seriously rather than dismissed as politically motivated, right-wing fanatics. For one thing, their claim is that they represent genuine, orthodox Christianity as preserved down through the ages. For another, they see themselves as part of that wider evangelical tradition that has had an honorable place in the church over the last three centuries. Most importantly, their proposals raise a number of fascinating questions that any comprehensive analysis of renewal must face. So in engaging the Fundamentalists, as represented by the leadership of the Southern Baptist tradition, we are taking on board much more than the suggestions of a small group in a large modern denomination. We are encountering the work of a whole phalanx of conservative Christians in the modern world.

How do the Fundamentalists see our current situation in the modern church? Their basic perception is that the church runs the risk of committing apostasy. They see the mainline Christian denominations in particular as being already well down that road, which explains their decline in membership. But numerical decline is not the main issue. The primary reality is that the churches of the West have systematically abandoned the gospel and are now reaping the consequences of their actions, as millions exit the old denominations and turn to more conservative brands of the faith. Such a turning is not an escapist mechanism to compensate for the loss of credibility in the modern world; it is the natural behavior of those who have gone in search of spiritual reality and have failed to find adequate nourishment in the central institutions that profess to provide it. Decline is the outcome of the erosion of the true gospel by the major churches of the West.

Decline is not, therefore, the result of some inevitable process of secularization. Indeed, there is no such inevitable process. Human beings are incurably religious creatures who will find fulfillment ultimately only in a relationship with God. Failing to secure this, they will seek refuge in other divinities, or they will turn in on themselves and seek salvation in merely secular reality. Decline, in this view, is a contingent historical reality that the churches have fostered or caused by failing to offer people the good news of the gospel in an uncompromising and full manner. Moreover, those who have championed secularization as somehow ineradicable have made illegitimate inferences from a particular cultural trend — as illustrated by events elsewhere in the world, where millions are becoming Christian. In addition, belief in the irresistible march of secularization rests on an unwarranted set of assumptions about human beings that have never been validated by scientific research but merely assumed as hidden metaphysical presuppositions. It depends, that is, on an unfounded commitment to a purely naturalist conception of human beings. Churches that have failed in these circumstances have done so because they have capitulated to the intellectual ideologies of the age. In short, they have committed apostasy.

How has this happened? Draper's analysis seeks to provide a considered answer. The root cause of the problem is that theologians have substituted reason for revelation as the foundation of the church's faith. They have abandoned the historic Christian position on the nature of the Bible, and the consequences for the life of the church are devastating. He laments,

> The Christian community in recent years has taken a drastic step in its theological commitment. Sometimes consciously, sometimes subconsciously, but always tragically, many professing Christians have slowly moved away from the historic positions concerning the nature of the Bible. Little or large, deliberate or not, when one takes such a step he courts disaster in his life and ministry. When one takes that tragic step the result is usually a loss of mission and evangelistic zeal; theological defection; undue emphasis upon the material and temporal with a corresponding loss of consciousness of the eternal; reliance upon mystical, personal truth; unjustified attachment to human reasoning — to name but a few spiritually destructive positions.[1]

The debate about the nature of Scripture is really an epistemological debate:

---

1. James T. Draper, Jr., *Authority: The Critical Issue for Southern Baptists* (Old Tappan, N.J.: Revell, 1984), p. 15.

The basic problem which we face today has to do with knowledge and truth. It is not the quantity of truth which is being debated, but the source of truth. Where does genuine truth originate, and how can we know that something is actually truth? This is the burning issue challenging every serious Bible student and Christian today. Philosophically, we refer to this whole area of study as epistemology.[2]

Our options in epistemology are limited to three. We can have rationalism, ecclesiastical authority, or divine revelation. The first, used deliberately as an umbrella term, is represented by reason, experience, and mysticism. The Roman Catholic Church represents the second. A divinely inspired Bible guaranteed by God's superintending action to be inerrant in the original autographs constitutes the third.

For Draper, commitment to biblical Christianity requires that we be clear that the third option is the only legitimate option for Christians in the Reformation tradition. In the end, critical inquiry requires that we have one fundamental base for all our theological deliberations. All claims must be validated by a transcendent norm. Once that norm is abandoned, there is no place to stop other than completely outside the Christian faith. In fact, anything else is an unstable position that will be carried to its logical conclusion by succeeding generations: "We must affirm the great Reformation doctrine of *sola scriptura*, Scripture only, as being our final, ultimate base of authority and truth. Anything less than that is deficient and opens the door to every conceivable kind of theological distortion."[3]

In Draper's account, the mainline churches have played out this basic scenario all too readily. Their primary mistake was to shift dramatically away from biblical authority, compromising time and again the internal security of their position. His interpretation reminds the reader of a castle surrounded by a moat that functions both as a defense and a source of water. A series of tunnels have been dug underneath the moat, allowing the enemy to enter and destroy the castle. Two factors exacer-

2. Draper, *Authority,* p. 16.
3. Draper, *Authority,* p. 22.

bate the situation. First, the enemies of the castle have their own water supplies, which, unbeknownst to the enemy, carry deadly poison. Sometimes water from an enemy tunnel seeps into the water in the moat, thus constantly threatening the purity of the castle's own water supply. Second, there is a constant risk that those appointed to protect the castle and to teach new generations about its wonderful treasures will unwittingly help the enemy gain access to the castle. This of course creates deep distrust, alienation, and even strife within the castle. The mere possibility of collaboration with the enemy keeps its inhabitants on edge. When leaders in the know suspect collaboration, real or imagined, the annual conventions of the castle become scenes of intense political maneuvering on all sides.

Draper identifies four distinct enemies at work contaminating the water supply. First, there is the application of historical approaches to the Scriptures. Not all critical work on Scripture is destructive, but clearly some is, notably form, redaction, and genre criticism. These have a place, if carefully used, but they easily become destructive when they are wedded to naturalistic or anti-supernaturalistic ways of seeing the world. A Hegelian, idealistic perspective also leads to faulty Bible study. A second enemy of the true faith is existential philosophy, which emerged on the heels of the Kant-cum-Schleiermacher revolution in philosophy and theology. It posits experience as the foundation of all theology, rejecting any recourse to propositional revelation. This constitutes a spectrum embracing Bultmann on the far left, Barth in the middle, and notable modern evangelicals on the right. The crucial problem in all these cases is that theology becomes subjective, mystical, and existential.

Draper's third source of trouble is naturalistic, uniformitarian science. Darwin, Freud, and Durkheim form a trio of enemies who cannot countenance the possibility of divine intervention, explaining everything in terms of universal, transtemporal laws and principles. Fourth and finally, there is the presumed contribution of comparative religion. In this case, Christianity is reduced to a culturally relative faith that has driven many away from traditional biblical theology.

Draper sums up the cumulative effects of these developments nicely:

These areas of concern represent a significant but mostly overlooked shift from divine revelation to rationalism as the ultimate base of authority. The destructive critics have shifted from revelation to reason. The naturalistic, uniformitarian scientists have shifted from revelation to reason. The philosophers have shifted from revelation to reason. The students of comparative religions, likewise. Ultimately, all these attacks have come because of the shift in the base of authority from revelation to reason.[4]

These developments cannot but entail disaster for the church both morally and theologically. They undercut in a deep way her evangelistic activity, because they deprive the latter of the biblical concepts of the human condition and the human response that constitute true evangelism.

What then should be done? The prescription is surely immediately in sight. The nub of the prescription is to get the church straight on the matter of authority. This has two radically different dimensions, one theological and one social. In the first place there has to be a return to the historic, biblical position of the church on the nature of the Bible. Here, Draper insists that throughout the history of the church, its leaders and theologians have held to a single account of biblical authority, even though verbally that account was expressed in diverse ways. From Clement of Rome through Luther and Calvin, to Edwards and Warfield, the church has always believed in the full inspiration and infallibility of the Bible. Likewise, within the history of the Baptist tradition, from John Smith and Thomas Helwys through Francis Wayland and John A. Broadus, down to W. T. Conner, Baptists have held to the inerrancy of Scripture in all that it says. This consensus is not surprising, because this is what the Bible teaches about itself. More importantly, it was what Jesus taught about Scripture. Hence, its denial is a frontal attack on the lordship of Christ over the believer.

The second, social dimension of authority is the more interesting and more controversial side of Draper's prescription. The crux of it is that Draper proposed that the Southern Baptist Convention develop a rule of

---

4. Draper, *Authority*, p. 42.

faith that would set theological parameters for its teachers, policymakers, and leaders. This was not an attempt to impose a creed on all Southern Baptists, and it was aimed at the convention level rather than the level of local membership. Such a move would take the convention to the point where it would define exactly what is meant by the gospel. It would not infringe on the cherished Baptist ideas of the priesthood of all believers, the sole competency of the individual, or the autonomy of the local church. It would not hinder legitimate diversity in the interpretation of Scripture among Baptists. It would not undercut the legitimate concept of academic freedom widely recognized in and for religious schools. And it would not mean a witch-hunt of current institutions in which moderates would be summarily ousted. In fact, Draper would be entirely satisfied if there were a balance of teachers in the seminaries of the Convention, so that those holding to the classical position would not be excluded by informal hiring policies. The proposed rule of faith would simply set boundaries for the leaders of the Southern Baptist Convention.

As to the content of the rule of faith, Draper suggested that it include the historic position of the church on Scripture, together with clauses affirming the deity and humanity of Christ, substitutionary atonement, the bodily resurrection of Jesus, and justification by faith. Distinctively Baptist beliefs, say, about immersion, might be added, but this and other matters could be left to a blue ribbon committee to discuss and bring to the Convention.[5] Draper essentially called for the recovery of the inerrancy of Scripture as the foundation of the church's theology, together with the drawing up of a creed that would be required as a condition of work by key figures in the Convention.

As we now know, this is not how things developed. Through a series of astute political moves, the Fundamentalists captured a commanding position in the Convention and have been able to achieve even more than Draper desired. They have now gotten control of the denomination. This development is hailed as a turnaround rare in the history of the Protestant tradition. As Timothy George states it, "For only the second

---

5. Draper provides a somewhat expanded list of items in the appendix to *Authority: The Critical Issue for Southern Baptists.*

time in this century, a major American denomination veering from its historical, evangelical roots has changed its trajectory."[6] The future ahead is one of internal institutional change and extensive consolidation. Central to this is a massive thrust outward in evangelism at home and abroad. Here renewal is not just a hope; it is already an embryonic and growing reality.

If Fundamentalists are concerned to restore the ancient faith of the church by recovering a particular doctrine of Scripture, charismatics focus on the recovery of a radical, fresh encounter with the Holy Spirit. Such a prescription involves a very different account of the problems of the church together with a different analysis of the causes at their root.

Initially, charismatics tend to focus on the needs of individual Christians rather than the church itself. Two images recur in the descriptions prevalent in the charismatic movement: one speaks of individual Christians being dry, the other of their being hungry. The former brings to mind the image of a person deprived of water; in a different mode, it makes one think of a land that has not seen rain for months on end. The second image brings to mind a person simply starving for food. In both cases, the individual already knows what it is to be alive and to have a normal supply of water and food. Somehow, however, the supply has been cut off, and a quiet desperation ensues; unless food and water are found and consumed, death is around the corner.

Both these images recur in Dennis Bennett's account of his pilgrimage. Bennett comes across as one of the last persons one would expect to see involved in the charismatic movement. As a boy, he had been brought from England to California. He had gone through a conventional conversion experience on the brink of his teenage years in the Christian Endeavor movement.[7] He went into the electronics industry, got married, and then at the age of twenty-six took off for the University of Chicago to prepare for the ministry. Reacting against the liberal humanism of his teachers, the professionalization of his relationship with

6. Timothy George, "The Southern Baptist Wars," *Christianity Today,* March 9, 1992, p. 24. The first to do this was the Missouri Synod Lutherans.

7. This was an international movement committed in local churches to the spiritual conversion and formation of young people.

God, the loss of his spiritual life that accompanied his training, and the vague beliefs of the church of his childhood, Bennett joined the Episcopal Church. He fully embraced the creeds, dogmas, and practices of the Anglo-Catholic tradition, and he settled happily into parish ministry. After sixteen years in the ministry, he faced a crisis: "I had a wonderful wife; I was successful in my work; yet I was dry and hungry deep inside."[8]

Intrigued by a young couple in his church who were not dry and hungry, Bennett began a search. He studied diligently in Scripture and tradition, he met and got to know intimately those who spoke winsomely of the power of the Holy Spirit in their lives, and he went through a lengthy process of deep soul-searching and prayer. After prolonged hesitation, Bennett eventually came to the conclusion that the deep problem in his own life and in the church he served was the absence of an encounter with the Holy Spirit. Both the early believers and those who currently manifested the kind of life Bennett was seeking had clear-cut experiences of receiving the power of the Holy Spirit. Further reception of this experience was accompanied by speaking in tongues. Eventually, he came secretly to desire this experience.

> I was like a starving man circling a table on which a delicious-looking feast is spread, watching the people seated at the table obviously enjoying the food, while trying to make up his mind whether it is really safe. . . . Finally, though, on a Saturday afternoon in November, after three whole months of circling, I said to my enthusiastic friends: "Look here, I've been reading my Bible, my Prayer Book, my theology books, my church history, and as far as I can see this experience you're talking about is in them all. I want what you've got! How do I get it?"[9]

Bennett was instructed to ask God for this experience, and others prayed for him as well. After praying quietly for about twenty minutes, he

---

8. Dennis J. Bennett, *Nine O'clock in the Morning* (London: Coverdale, 1970), p. 27.
9. Bennett, *Nine O'clock*, pp. 35-36.

spoke in tongues. Then, after four days of further meditation and seeking, he records the following experience:

> Once more I prayed very quietly and cautiously, and this time, after only about three or four minutes, words began to come in another language, the same language, I noted that I had spoken in the previous Saturday — at least it sounded like it. . . . But as I spoke on, something else began to happen. My heart began to get happier and happier! The presence of God that was so clearly seen in earlier days to be the real reason for living suddenly enveloped me again after the many, many years of dryness. Never had I experienced God's presence in such reality as now. It might have frightened me except that I recognized that this was the same Presence of the Lord that I had sensed when I first accepted Jesus, and that I had known when I used to get up early during my years in the business world; only the intensity and reality of my present experience was far greater than anything I had believed possible. If those earlier experiences were the flashbulbs, this was as if someone had suddenly turned on the floodlights! The reality of God was something that I had felt all the way through — even with my body. But instead of being fearful, I felt tremendously happy and elated.[10]

Thus began a radically new phase of Bennett's life and ministry. In due course he identified a whole series of consequent changes both in himself and in others. Chief among these we should mention the following: a fresh interest in and understanding of the Scriptures, a new delight in worship, a gradual recovery of the gifts of healing and prophecy, a passion for holiness of life, a sense of daily, particular providence, a desire and ability to spread the good news of God's love and power, an empowerment of laity for ministry, and a new sense of the reality of radical evil in the church and the world. Not everything was smooth sailing; Bennett faced opposition from colleagues in ministry and from his parish church, so much so that he resigned and took up work in a kind of mission

---

10. Bennett, *Nine O'clock*, pp. 39-41.

church in Ballard, a suburb of Seattle. Moreover, his wife died after a long battle with cancer. Yet in the long run he became something of an international celebrity, traveling across the world to speak of his newfound faith and freedom.

Implicit in his narrative is a clear analysis of the problems of the modern church together with the fundamental solution to those problems. The basic problem is an unawareness of and subsequent absence of baptism in the Holy Spirit; this is the cause of dryness and hunger among Christians. The solution is for Christian people in their own time and place to enter into a fresh and ongoing baptism of the Holy Spirit. Bennett is reserved in pressing the matter theologically. Indeed, there is a marked ambivalence in the way he speaks of the issue. First, nowhere does Bennett say that speaking in tongues is the exclusive or even initial evidence of the experience of baptism in the Holy Spirit, yet he rarely mentions the latter without noting that it is accompanied by speaking in tongues. As he puts it modestly but firmly, "It came with the package."[11] Second, Bennett wobbles back and forth between saying that Christians receive the Holy Spirit in the baptism of the Holy Spirit and saying that in the baptism of the Holy Spirit, Christians make themselves available to the Holy Spirit.[12] Towards the end, he describes the matter in this way:

> Once again the miracle began to happen, as Christians, already indwelt by the Holy Spirit, began to trust Jesus to inundate them by his power and freedom, so that the riches stored in them could break forth to the world. One after another, some hesitatingly, some fluently, they began to speak in new languages.[13]

This ambivalence is played out in later developments in the charismatic movement when a variety of theological frameworks are invoked in accounting for baptism in the Holy Spirit. However, this in no way shows that charismatics are unclear about the central issue in renewal. What is needed, they insist, is the baptism and filling of the Holy Spirit.

11. This is the title to Chapter 3.
12. See the relevant footnotes on pp. 106, 146.
13. Bennett, *Nine O'clock*, p. 171.

From this flows the freedom, the power for witness and service, the love, and the gifts that are essential if the church is to do what God requires of her in the modern world.

What help can we gain from the Fundamentalists and charismatics, as represented here? What elements in their deliberations provide genuine medicine for the modern church? Changing the metaphor to that of journey and pilgrimage, are there any items here that ought to be stored with the luggage as we move forward? I would like to focus particularly on the territory that the proposals occupy.

The Fundamentalists clearly see the elemental problem of the church as intellectual and theological. More precisely, they are betting the future on a very particular epistemology of theology. The solution offered, however, is wildly off base. For one, the whole attempt to secure the kind of formally approved foundations required is precisely the heart of the whole Enlightenment project. Hence, contemporary Fundamentalists are thoroughly modern creatures committed to the same intellectual aspirations as their secular enemies. If the Enlightenment has caused so much trouble, it would be odd in the extreme to argue that we could get beyond it by accepting its basic premises and modes of operation. Second, as I have argued at length elsewhere, the Fundamentalist doctrine of Scripture is deeply flawed. The crucial weakness is that it has historically depended on a doctrine of divine dictation or on a latent confusing of divine inspiration with divine speaking and related speech acts of God.[14] Thirdly, and most importantly, the move to include the inerrancy of Scripture as the linchpin in a new creed for the church involves not only a radical departure from the actual canonical decisions of the church as made in the great ecumenical councils but also a profound reorientation of the inner structure of the church's intellectual heritage and vision. It involves a shift from soteriology to epistemology.

What is fascinating about the basic proposal as it emanates from the Baptist tradition is the fact that it highlights the importance of canonical decisions for the identity and well-being of the church. The conservatives

---

14. William J. Abraham, *The Divine Inspiration of Holy Scripture* (Oxford: Oxford University Press, 1981).

are correct to see that the church needs markers of intellectual identity. Frankly, churches cannot long survive without some kind of rule of faith. Such a discovery is particularly ironic coming from the heart of the Baptist tradition, which for generations has lauded autonomy, freedom, soul competency, the priesthood of all believers, and the like in such a way as to reject the place of agreed and functioning canons of the church's doctrine. The reworking of the Baptist tradition so that it can come to terms with reality is surely salutary and timely.

Yet this positive direction is flawed in several ways. First, it is acted on only halfheartedly. The matter is not thought through either historically or systematically. It strikes one as deeply incoherent, although there is plenty of precedent in the Protestant tradition to follow in this respect. Second, the proposal conflates and confuses canons of ecclesial identity with norms of epistemology, thus offering stones when one asks for bread. Conversely, it offers bread where one needs cement. The church needs doctrinal and other materials and practices to hold it together across time and space. Third, Draper and his friends depend on a superficial reading of the intellectual debates of the modern period. Even their reading of the evangelical tradition is too wooden to capture the highways and byways of this honorable movement.

That epistemological concerns of the kind identified by the Fundamentalists are an entirely secondary matter is surely borne out by Bennett's pilgrimage. If there is a key to renewal, then it is to be found where Bennett locates it. Time will tell, as we proceed through this volume, whether this conviction can be sustained. For now, we record that the foundation of the church's life is to be found by exploring to the full the riches of God made incarnate in Jesus Christ through the agency of the Holy Spirit here and now. The canons of the church in Scripture, creed, liturgy, and the like provide the context for such an exploration. They are not some grand epistemological framework of the kind envisaged by Draper; they are the normal means of grace given by God to the church. Even then, what one needs to start with is not some grand theory of their nature and function. As Bennett shows, he was thoroughly confused initially about the nature of his problem and how to solve it. What is essential is a sense of need, a deep humility, and a radical openness to meet and receive from the living God. This is where all renewal must begin and end. The church and her rich canonical traditions simply provide the context where this can happen.

Moreover, Bennett is right to tread warily in spelling out theologically exactly how we are to articulate the relevant doctrine of the activity of the Holy Spirit. We must surely speak about being baptized and filled with the Holy Spirit. All three Synoptic Gospels insist that this was why Christ came. He came not merely to die and rise, but to baptize the people of God in the Holy Spirit.[15] This is precisely what is represented by Pentecost. Moreover, there is abundant evidence in the history and phenomenology of Christian experience to show that this is an ongoing reality in the church down through the ages. So any theology that bypasses this has missed the mark. Yet it is an open question how this is to be integrated into the great themes of Christian theology, as the subsequent history of the charismatic movement makes only too clear.

An analogy will help. In 1738, John Wesley had an encounter with God at Aldersgate that his disciples and friends have often identified as his conversion. In recent years, this interpretation has been contested on several fronts. Some see it as a vocational crisis, and some just as one more experience in Wesley's relationship with God. Richard Heitzenrater, in my view, has correctly unraveled the mystery.[16] At Aldersgate, Wesley was trying out the theology of the Moravians as it applied to Christian experience. Immediately after Aldersgate, Wesley accepted the interpretation supplied by the Moravians. However, subsequent experience and reflection made it clear that the Moravians were wrong. Wesley had to redescribe his experience and rework his theology in such a way as to separate the wheat from the chaff. We know what the wheat was: Wesley had discovered the work of the Holy Spirit in assurance. It took years to work this out. Even yet, whole tracts of the church do not know of this rich gift of the Holy Spirit.

Likewise, Bennett is right to insist that baptism in the Holy Spirit is

15. Matthew 3:11, Mark 1:8, Luke 3:16.
16. Richard Heitzenrater, "Great Expectations: Aldersgate and the Evidences of Genuine Christianity," in Heitzenrater, *Mirror and Memory* (Nashville: Kingswood, 1989), pp. 106-49.

central to the renewal of the church. We have only begun, however, to fathom what this may mean both theologically and practically. It may take us a very long time to come to terms with this in even a minimally adequate way. We have not, of course, said a word on how all of this might be related to the challenges of the Enlightenment. This is a topic that we will begin to engage in the next chapter.

CHAPTER 3

A TALE OF TWO BISHOPS

LESSLIE NEWBIGIN AND JOHN SHELBY SPONG

IN THIS CHAPTER I WILL explore and examine two contrasting proposals that have been developed by two world-famous bishops. The first is
that provided by Bishop Lesslie Newbigin (1909-1998), the second by
Bishop John Shelby Spong (1931-). In both cases I shall provide some
brief background information, then I shall outline their respective positions. In the last section I shall make some comparative comments.

Bishop Lesslie Newbigin has been one of the most respected recent
commentators on the current state and fate of Christianity in the West.
Newbigin was something of an elder statesman of the ecumenical movement. He was the first director of the World Council of Churches' Division of World Mission and Evangelism. He served the church with distinction in India and returned to retirement in England in the mid-1970s
only to find that the country he had left earlier was now in desperate need
of re-evangelization. Newbigin was one of those few figures that have
risen to distinction in no less than two distinct church bodies. He was a
bishop in the Church of South India for twenty-seven years, and in 1978-
79 he was the moderator of the United Reformed Church in England.

Over the years Newbigin has written a spate of books that have had a
lasting impact on mission theory in the modern church. In more recent
years, much of his time was given to pondering the needs and problems
of the churches in the West, especially in Britain. When he arrived in Birmingham after his distinguished ministry in India, he quickly discovered

that there were several crucial matters that needed attention. He threw himself eagerly into debates about the nature of missionary training in the modern world, about the possibility of an unpaid ministry of word and sacrament, about the nature of religious education in a multicultural city, about the imperative to take the gospel to all the world, about the closing of local churches in tough inner-city areas, and the like. These encounters led Newbigin to take a long, hard look at the church in the West.

A moving point of entry into Newbigin's thinking about the prospects for the church in the West can be found in the penultimate chapter of his memoirs. In 1979, Newbigin found himself presiding over the Birmingham District Council of the United Reformed Church. In the course of the meeting, they had to face the possibility of closing an old church outside Winson Green prison. Newbigin could not contemplate such a decision. In the end, he became the pastor on a part-time basis.

> On 2 January I was duly installed and since then I have been struggling to fulfill the obligations of this ministry. It is much harder than anything I met in India. There is a cold contempt for the gospel which is harder to face than opposition. As I visit the Asian homes in the district, most of them Sikhs or Hindus, I find a welcome which is often denied on the doorsteps of the natives. I have been forced to recognize that the most difficult missionary frontier in the contemporary world is the one of which the Churches have been — on the whole — so little conscious, the frontier that divides the world of biblical faith from the world whose values and beliefs are ceaselessly fed into every home on the television screen. Like others I had been accustomed, especially in the 1960s, to speak of England as a secular society. I have now come to realize that I was the easy victim of an illusion from which my reading of the Gospels should have saved me. No room remains empty for long. If God is driven out, the gods come trooping in. *England is a pagan society and the development of a truly missionary encounter with this very tough form of paganism is the greatest intellectual and practical task facing the church.*[1]

1. Lesslie Newbigin, *Unfinished Agenda* (London: SPCK, 1985), p. 249 (emphasis in the original).

Newbigin's description of the current ecclesial scene is not a happy one. Three components are worth mentioning. First, there has been widespread decline in the membership of the church, so much so that the church, at least in England, faces a new paganism. It is ill prepared to do so with conviction and flair. Second, the great effort to bring about visible unity between the various denominations has not succeeded. Many in the West see the World Council of Churches as a threat in that it tends to focus aggressively on justice for the poor and the oppressed. Moreover, a new generation has emerged who do not share the great ecumenical vision of the postwar years, and who tend to work primarily from within their ecclesiastical ghettos. Third, over the years there has developed a deep breach between those who broadly see themselves as evangelical and those who see themselves as ecumenical. This has led to a tragic separation within the Western church, a separation that was exacerbated by the swing from a focus on secularity in the 1960s to a focus on spirituality in the 1970s. Overall, Newbigin paints a picture of massive failure: failure in unity and failure in mission, the two great pillars of the ecumenical movement.

His most recent work represents an extended attempt to unravel the etiology of this state of affairs. It involves a foray into the upper echelons of European intellectual history. No less than four books are devoted to this exercise.[2]

Newbigin traces the roots of the problems of the modern church right back to the middle of the eighteenth century. What happened then was a radical break from the Christian civilization which had held society together virtually since the days of Augustine. As we all know, the watchword of the new movement that ultimately swept through Europe from top to bottom was that of "Enlightenment." The rise of science precipitated a series of crises for the classical Christian traditions. It led to a new theory of knowledge that exalted doubt over faith, that is, of reason over

2. Lesslie Newbigin, *The Other Side of 1984: Questions For the Churches* (Geneva: World Council of Churches, 1984), *Foolishness to the Greeks: The Gospel and Western Culture* (Grand Rapids: Eerdmans, 1986), *The Gospel in a Pluralist Society* (Grand Rapids: Eerdmans, 1989), and *Truth To Tell: The Gospel as Public Truth* (Geneva: World Council of Churches, 1991).

superstition, and to the conscious adoption of critical method over an arbitrary commitment to special revelation. This new theory looked upon the natural sciences as the paradigm of all knowledge. It also led in due course to a split between the world of facts and the world of values. The former were ascertained by science and were to be universally believed; the latter included everything else, but most especially metaphysical, religious and moral proposals, and all these were entirely a matter of private choice and personal opinion.

The Enlightenment also created a new theory of the state. The nation-state replaced the church and the empire as the centerpiece of the political scene. Its job in part was to hold the ring between competing or pluralistic conceptions of the public good, eschewing any deep theory of the good life. The state staked its authority on its objective neutrality above the contesting parties together with the informed analysis of the bureaucratic procedures essential to the running of the public order. The chief alternative to this was worked out in Marxism. In this case, the commitment to a scientific analysis of society was wedded to an apocalyptic utopianism that swept through the world until it began unraveling at the end of the 1980s.

The Enlightenment also involved a new account of economics that cut economic affairs loose from moral considerations by insisting on the supremacy of economic laws. It created, moreover, a new ethic that focused on the pursuit of happiness. The language of rights arose to usurp the language of duties, creating in turn mass movements of protest and reform that are still very much with us in the form of feminism and multiculturalism. In the end, the Enlightenment really created a whole new conception of the human person. Persons are to be understood as autonomous individuals who best fulfill their destiny by rejecting dogma, tradition, and authority, and by exercising reason as suitably informed by scientific experts.

Christianity, insofar as it existed, became in these circumstances an entirely private affair. Individually, it took the form of an intense personal experience of God with nothing to say in the public arena. Corporately, it took the form of diverse denominations. The proliferation of denominations reflected in fact the domestication of the Christian gospel.

Denominations were permitted by the nation state as a privileged private option. They merely represented the nation's collective private choices; hence they could do nothing to challenge the initial secularism and eventual paganism of the public order.

The church in the West developed the problems that currently beset it by entering into a marriage with this complex cultural reality. Newbigin writes:

> It would be hard to deny that contemporary British (and most Western) Christianity is in an advanced state of syncretism. The Church has lived so long as a permitted and even privileged minority, accepting regulation to the private sphere in a culture whose public vision is controlled by a totally different vision of reality, that it has almost lost the power to address a radical challenge to that vision and therefore to "modern Western civilization" as a whole.[3]

This syncretism is manifest not just in the inability of the church to speak to issues in the public domain; it is also visible in the internal theological developments of Western Christian theology. Thus the great hero of much Western theology in the modern period is Friedrich Schleiermacher, who surrendered the great dogmas of the faith, like the doctrines of the Incarnation and Trinity, by making the religious affections of the heart rather than the great events of historic divine revelation the center of Christian reality. It is also visible in the move to make the resurrection of Christ a psychological event in the lives of the disciples rather than a real event of new creation in the midst of human history. Syncretism is also manifest in the inability of biblical scholars to get beyond the disposition to see the Bible as anything other than one more item of our cultural heritage. Thus theologians are inherently incapable of providing a substantial critique of our present cultural situation.

All this is relatively familiar material. What is new is the particular twist that Newbigin gives to his diagnosis of the ills of the modern church. Virtually everything that has gone wrong in both Western cul-

---

3. Newbigin, *The Other Side of 1984*, p. 23 (emphasis mine).

ture and the Western church can be traced to a single epistemological shift at the beginning of the modern world. Drawing on the work of Michael Polanyi, he thinks that the really deep problem is a shift in what he calls "fiduciary frameworks." The problem with the whole Enlightenment project (and the Western church insofar as it has followed it) is that it bought the impossible notion that there could be any knowledge without faith. The reverse, as Augustine saw so clearly, is the actual truth about the attainment of knowledge. All knowledge ultimately rests on dogma, on faith, on a fiduciary framework that cannot be proved. The real enemy then is Descartes. Descartes turned away from faith in God and developed a radical method of doubt that made skepticism the foundation of all claims to truth.

Not surprisingly, the beginning point of the solution to our problems is to develop a better epistemological framework for the life of the church:

> What is now being proposed is that not just in the private world but also in the public world another model for understanding is needed; that this in turn requires the acknowledgment that our most fundamental beliefs cannot be demonstrated but are held by faith; that it is the responsibility of the Church to offer this new model of understanding as the basis for the radical renewal of our culture; and that without such radical renewal our culture has no future. This is — if we may put it very sharply — an invitation to recover a proper acknowledgment of the role of dogma. It is an invitation to the Church to be bold in offering to men and women of our culture a way of understanding which makes no claim to be demonstrable in the terms of "modern" thought, which is not "scientific" in the popular sense of the word, which is based unashamedly on the revelation of God made in Jesus Christ and attested in scripture and the tradition of the Church, and which is offered as a fresh starting point for the exploration of the mystery of human existence and for coping with its practical tasks not only in the private and domestic life of the believers but also in the public life of the citizen.[4]

4. Newbigin, *The Other Side of 1984*, p. 27. Compare the following statement: "a fifth area of questioning will concern assumptions about what is involved in knowing. *This is*

From this fountain flows practically everything else that Newbigin has to say about the logistics of ecclesial renewal. His strategy is in fact self-consciously elitist in character. He calls for a new missionary encounter with modern Western culture led by an army of lay Christians, who will enter the diverse dimensions of modern culture and challenge the reigning ideology in the name of the truth of the gospel. This will entail a double immersion. On the one hand, it requires an immersion in the Christian faith. On the other hand, it requires immersion in the world of economics, education, law, politics, science, the media, and the like. These engagements will, in turn, require a new rendering of the relation between the churches and the political order. Newbigin calls this relation "committed pluralism." Committed pluralism rejects both the idea of a Constantinian theocracy and of an agnostic pluralism, opting instead for a resolute commitment to Christ as Lord over Caesar in which dissident alternatives will be given freedom to live and work. As for the church at large, Newbigin calls for a laundry list of changes. He calls her to recover her catholic face, unashamedly confessing her faith in the historic reality of God's special revelation in the rescue of Israel from Egypt and in the events concerning the man Jesus of Nazareth. He calls for a robust faith in the resurrection, in the independence and authority of the church's narrative identity as found in Scripture and tradition, and in the dogmas of the Incarnation and the Trinity. Finally he highlights the need for a radical conversion where we turn and enter the kingdom of God here and now and become active members of local congregations as the embodiment of the church universal.

Was Newbigin an optimist or a pessimist as he looked ahead into the future? My distinct impression is that he was a pessimist. He sounds bleak about the future of the ecumenical movement, although he had lots of enthusiasm about the future of the church outside the West. He was very unhappy with the current political scene, showing little eagerness to support the principles and policies represented by Ronald Reagan and Margaret Thatcher in the 1980s, and more recently by George Bush and

---

our most fundamental task, because the ways of knowing developed by modern science since the seventeenth century are fundamental to our western culture" (Newbigin, *The Other Side of 1984*, p. 60, emphasis mine).

Tony Blair. Some critics see him as a sophisticated Fundamentalist who does little more that wage a weak, rearguard attack against the steamroller of modernity and postmodernity. Yet his prescience has been uncanny at times. He wistfully suggested on one occasion that just as Marxism was really the religion of the twentieth century, so Islam would be the religion of the twenty-first century.[5] To be sure, Newbigin was a man of incredible energy and extraordinary goodwill. He was an ecclesiastical statesman of the highest order, a prince of the church in the twentieth century.[6] He was a man of persistent faith who would not be perturbed in any ultimate way if the church failed to make its way forward in the West. Yet the tone of his work was increasingly somber and cautious. One senses that he believed that all was not well as he contemplated the future; and he would not, therefore, be surprised if things get a lot worse before they get better.

A very different voice in renewal is represented by the fourth figure I want to review in this tour of proposals about renewal. I have in mind the suggestions developed in a whole series of books by Bishop John Shelby Spong of the Episcopal Church, U.S.A. Bishop Spong is a familiar face across the English-speaking world, so much so that I can limit my comments to what is absolutely essential.

Spong is a formidable figure in person. He is a brilliant orator and communicator. He has no trouble holding his own with Donahue, O'Reilly, and other television anchors; and his ability to make use of the press and the publishers to get out his message is awesome. Many of these rhetorical skills were honed over the years in his journey from Fundamentalism to radicalism, and in his journey from a parish priest to a nationally famous bishop, and then on to a self-styled public intellectual. He outlines that journey with great verve in his fine autobiography *Here I Stand: My Struggle for a Christianity of Integrity, Love, and Equality.*[7] Even those who detest Spong's theology and despise what they take to be his

---

5. I owe this to personal conversation.

6. In personal conversation I have heard some affectionately refer to him as a "Father" of the modern church.

7. John Shelby Spong, *Here I Stand: My Struggle for a Christianity of Integrity, Love, and Equality* (San Francisco: HarperCollins, 1999).

maverick style cannot but be moved by his battle to work his way out of Fundamentalism, by his resolute stand on civil rights in the 1960s, by his efforts to combat racism, by his total commitment to the labors of a parish priest, and by his very difficult domestic situation. He has had his fair share of hard-hitting critics. One showed up at his first wife's funeral. Spong recalls,

> While seated with my daughters in the first pew of St. Paul's Church beside Joan's pall-draped coffin, I was amazed to feel myself being struck across the back of my shoulders with a cane in a manner that was clearly not accidental. My assailant was an elderly woman. I turned instinctively to respond to this blow. This woman then said, in a voice audible to anyone within ten yards, "You son of a bitch." Continuing her journey down the aisle, she went through the side door with the pallbearers, all but one of whom were priests of our diocese, who were waiting to come into the church. To them she said, "I've been wanting to tell that bastard what I think of him for a long time, and I finally got the chance." She then disappeared from my life to live in the shadows of anonymity forever.[8]

The best place to find Spong's views on renewal is in his 1998 book *Why Christianity Must Change or Die: A Bishop Speaks to Believers in Exile*.[9] Supplementary to that we can add his William Belden Noble Lectures at Harvard Divinity School that are published as *A New Christianity for a New World: Why Traditional Faith is Dying and How a New Faith is Being Born*.[10]

We can make our way into Spong's mind by picking up the interesting metaphor buried in the subtitle *Why Christianity Must Change or Die*. We find ourselves, he says, "in the wilderness." Later he draws on a metaphor in the neighborhood of that of wilderness: we are in "exile." His concern

---

8. Spong, *Here I Stand*, p. 354.

9. John Shelby Spong, *Why Christianity Must Change or Die: A Bishop Speaks to Believers in Exile* (San Francisco: HarperCollins, 1998).

10. John Shelby Spong, *A New Christianity for a New World: Why Traditional Faith is Dying and How a New Faith is Being Born* (San Francisco: HarperCollins, 2001).

is with "believers in exile."[11] He bears a pastoral responsibility for "that silent majority of believers who find it increasingly difficult to remain members of the Church and still be thinking people."[12] More specifically his burden is for those who can no longer recite the creeds with honesty. The Apostle's Creed, the Nicene Creed, the Chalcedonian definition, all these need revisiting, especially "if those so-literalized words prove to be no longer capable of leading into the experience of God toward which they originally pointed."[13] Speaking personally, he writes,

> While claiming to be a believer, and still asserting my deeply held commitment to Jesus as Lord and Christ, I also recognize that I live in a state of exile from the presuppositions of my own religious past. I am exiled from the literal understanding that shaped the creed at its creation. I am exiled from the worldview in which the creed was formed.[14]

We can see immediately the terrain on which Bishop Spong is camped. It is an intellectual terrain. The fundamental problem of the church is intellectual; it is wedded to a set of intellectual commitments that are no longer believable and that distort the original intention behind their creation, namely, the articulation of the experience of God of the early generations of Christians. The problem is one of intellectual honesty and integrity. Here is how he spells this out in terms of exile and wilderness:

> I begin by stating the obvious. Exile is never a voluntary experience. It is always something forced upon a person or a people by things or circumstances over which the affected ones have no control. One does not leave one's values, one's way of life, or one's defining beliefs voluntarily.
>
> The second fact is that exile is not a wilderness through which one journeys to arrive at a promised land. Exile is an enforced dislo-

11. Spong, *Why Christianity Must Change or Die,* p. xvii.
12. Spong, *Why Christianity Must Change or Die,* p. 4.
13. Spong, *Why Christianity Must Change or Die,* p. 19.
14. Spong, *Why Christianity Must Change or Die,* p. 20.

cation into which one enters without any verifiable hope of either a return to the past or an arrival at some future desired place.

I have quite specifically chosen this exile image to describe the state of faith in our postmodern world. I do so because the concept of exile is a familiar word in the sacred history of the Jewish and Christian people. Our spiritual ancestors have been there before. They indeed called a specific and defining moment in their faith journey "the Exile." An examination of this critical time in our religious past might help us to embrace our present situation. It might also provide us with insight into our own religious future, if there is to be a future.[15]

Spong goes on to recount the familiar story of the exile. It is the deployment of that analogy that is pivotal for our purposes. The crux of the matter is this. Just as the Jewish faith fell apart for those transported to Babylonian exile, so the Christian faith has fallen apart for those transported into the intellectual world of modernity. Belief in the personal God of Christianity became impossible as we found ourselves in the world of Nicolaus Copernicus, Galileo Galilei, Isaac Newton, Charles Darwin, Sigmund Freud, Carl Jung, Albert Einstein, and Carl Sagan. Spong lays out the parallels with exquisite rhetorical skill:

These Jews once believed that God fought at their side against the enemies. They could believe that no longer. They once believed that God might punish them for their waywardness but that God would not destroy them. They could believe that no longer. They once believed they were a specially chosen people. They believed that no longer. They once believed that God instructed them on where to live and how to worship. They could believe that no longer. They once believed that God dwelled in Jerusalem and ruled over Judah. They could believe that no longer. They once believed that God could hear their prayers. They could believe that no longer. They once believed they had a destiny and a future. They could believe that no longer.

15. Spong, *Why Christianity Must Change or Die*, pp. 22-23.

They once believed that God would care for them. They could believe that no longer.

They could not sing the Lord's song again, for they were in a strange and devastating exile, and in that exile the God they had once served lost all meaning. This God, quite frankly, could no longer be God for them. It is traumatic to watch the God who has given shape, definition, and meaning to life be removed from a people's awareness. There are but two alternatives for such a displaced deity. This God must either grow or die. That is what being in spiritual exile is all about:[16]

The God of our traditional past, who was the source of our values, the definer of our sense of right and wrong, was simply no more. We, like the Jews of old, have been forcefully removed from all that previously had given life meaning. The God we once worshipped had been obliterated before our eyes. We no longer knew who God was or who we were. We knew that we were in exile, even if we did not possess the words to describe that state of life. That is, I am convinced, where the formerly Christian western world lives today. Some will surely deny it. Others will try to ignore it. None, however, will escape it. No way out of this exile is either visible or guaranteed. We are forced to recognize that other gods have died in human history before this generation. No altars are today erected anywhere to Baal, Astarte, Molech, Re, Jupiter, Zeus, Mars, or Mithra. We wonder if deicide is happening again, only now to our God.[17]

What then of a solution? Spong is at once cautious and sharp at this juncture. The sharpness flits around his clear convictions about what is no longer possible for us: there can be no return to Fundamentalism or orthodoxy. He is absolutely adamant on this point. Yet, as perhaps someone in exile is likely to be, he is cautious about moving on, for he is unsure where to go. This may be one reason why he has resolutely insisted on re-

16. Spong, *Why Christianity Must Change or Die*, pp. 28-29.
17. Spong, *Why Christianity Must Change or Die*, p. 40.

maining a bishop and continuing to minister within the Episcopal Church. Compare this with, say, Rudolf Bultmann, on whom Spong is to some extent dependent. Bultmann was very clear that in his revisions of the Christian faith and in his rejection of direct divine action in the world, say, in miracle, he was sure he was actually recovering the intention of the gospel and the New Testament.[18] Bultmann's was a journey backwards to recover what he took to be the faith of the church at the beginning of its journey. Spong has no interest in going back. His journey is to the future, and the arena he must occupy is clear. Given that his diagnosis is centered on matters of creed and of belief, his solution has to be in this domain. And that is exactly where we find his positive alternative. His fundamental move is to work on a radical revision of the content of Christian belief so that Christianity might be intellectually credible in a new day. At this point, he turns for inspiration to an earlier generation of theologians and scholars, notably to the work of Dietrich Bonhoeffer in Germany, John Robinson in England, and Paul Tillich in North America. His crucial revision is to insist that we must now develop an appropriate discourse that will capture our contemporary experience of ultimate reality in a way that is in keeping with the central intellectual and moral presuppositions of our time. His strategy is to work though the themes of the creed, discarding what is outworn and outdated, keeping the relevant experience that lies at their base, and then reaching for a new way to articulate our faith today. He supplies us with a fulsome summary of the outcome:

1.   Theism, as a way of defining God, is dead. God can no longer be understood with credibility as a Being, supernatural in power, dwelling above the sky and prepared to invade human history periodically to enforce the divine will. So, most theological God-talk is meaningless unless we find a new way to speak of God.

2.   Since God can no longer be conceived in theistic terms, it becomes nonsensical to seek to understand Jesus as the incarnation of the theistic deity. So, the Christology of the ages is bankrupt.

---

18. Rudolf Bultmann, "New Testament and Mythology," in Bultmann, *Kerygma and Myth* (New York: Harper and Row, 1961), pp. 1-44.

3. The biblical story of the perfect and finished creation from which human beings fell into sin is pre-Darwinian mythology and post-Darwinian nonsense.

4. The virgin birth, understood as literal biology, makes the divinity of Christ, as traditionally understood, impossible.

5. The miracle stories of the New Testament can no longer be interpreted in a post-Newtonian world as supernatural events performed by an incarnate deity.

6. The view of the cross as the sacrifice of the sins of the world is a barbarian idea based on the primitive concepts of God that must be dismissed.

7. Resurrection is an action of God, who raised Jesus into the meaning of God. It therefore cannot be a physical resuscitation occurring inside human history.

8. The story of the ascension assumed a three-tiered universe and is therefore not capable of being translated into the concepts of the post-Copernican space age.

9. There is no external, objective, revealed standard writ in Scripture or on tablets of stone that will govern our ethical behavior for all time.

10. Prayer cannot be a request made to a theistic deity to act in a human way in human history in a particular way.

11. The hope of life after death must be separated forever from the church behavior-control mentality of reward and punishment. The Church must abandon, therefore, its reliance on guilt as a motivator of behavior.

12. All human beings bear God's image and must be respected for what each person is. Therefore, no external description of one's being, whether based on race, ethnicity, gender, or sexual orientation, can properly be used as the basis for either rejection or discrimination.[19]

Now that we have summarized the alternatives posed by Newbigin and Spong, we are in a position to take stock once again of what is at issue in the renewal of the church. On the surface it looks as if we have two

19. Appendix B, pp. 453-54 of Spong, *Here I Stand*.

radically different proposals here. Below the surface, however, it is clear that Newbigin and Spong share a common orientation. Both think that the fundamental problem is intellectual in nature. Here, surprisingly, they occupy the same terrain as is staked out by the Fundamentalist James Draper. All three are in search of an adequate epistemology of theology. Draper finds it in an inerrant Bible; Newbigin finds it in a form of fideism inspired by Michael Polanyi; Spong finds it in religious experience. The shared assumption at this point is that if we can only get straight on our theory of knowledge and the appropriate doctrine that can be derived from it, we will be well on our way in renewal. We saw how dubious this was in the case of Draper earlier. There is a very good reason to extend our doubts to include Newbigin and Spong. Neither the gospel nor the deep intellectual content of the Christian faith are a theory of knowledge. They are constituted by the good news that God has entered the world to heal it through the work of his Son in the power of the Holy Spirit. It is surely a radical mistake to think that this depends on any particular philosophical theory designed to resolve long-standing questions about rationality, justification, and knowledge. Yet this is exactly what Newbigin and Spong assume. Newbigin, to be sure, is more forthright and explicit about his theory of knowledge, and he deploys it to protect that classical faith of the church. Spong is much more amateurish in his philosophical commitments, and he is clearly more interested in the deconstruction of the classical faith of the church than he is in coming to terms with the problems of epistemology. However, the deep worry that drives them both is for the credibility of the gospel today. This is where they believe the heavy lifting has to be done in renewal.

Clearly, there is some point to this worry. Both insiders and outsiders to the Christian faith have a host of intellectual questions that deserve attention. It is easy to be gripped by worries about credibility and truth. Christian evangelists and teachers at their best have always recognized this. They have not been diffident about developing various forms of apologetics to address the objections to belief that inevitably crop up. Thus we can readily agree that there is a place in the renewal of the church for addressing problems and queries. In due course I shall indicate how they may be tackled with flair. However, the Christian faith is not in itself a philosophical program. It is something much deeper. Moreover, there is an element of ineradicable mystery in the gospel and in the doctrines that have been inspired by it. Thus there is the constant danger not just that the faith will be sidelined and marginalized by the philosophical ideas developed to protect it, but also that the faith will be set aside in order to safeguard the intellectual constructs developed to defend it.

Newbigin manages to avoid this pitfall; Spong does not. What saves Newbigin at this point is his resolute grounding in the faith of the church prior to the great schism of the eleventh century and his long experience in taking the gospel to an alien culture. Spong has no such grounding or experience. Converted within the boundaries of modern Fundamentalism, he has never really recovered from the thinness of its doctrines or the narrowness of its structures. The marks of the former Fundamentalism in his preaching and teaching are obvious. There is the same sense of alienation from tradition, the same angry self-assurance, the same hunger for intellectual and scholarly recognition, the same boundless evangelistic energy for the cause, the same pretentious self-importance, the same note of apocalyptic urgency, and the same faith in simple, sure-fire arguments that will shoot down the opposition in flames.

Fundamentalism has one redeeming feature. There is still enough of the faith left within it to convert the seeker; there is enough glimmer of gospel light to bring many to God. With Spong even this is now gone. While his ideas are cleverly presented as the best of the best of contemporary theology, they are really a repackaging of a position that was worked out in Europe and in North America in the 1950s and 1960s. They reflect the secularism and disaffection of the period. Listening to Spong is like revisiting an old movie where the color has faded and the sound has become crackly and crabby. Not surprisingly, former or dissatisfied Fundamentalists welcome him as a breath of fresh air. Atheism and agnosticism are too difficult for many of them; Spong provides a way whereby they can still be religious without being either Fundamentalist or atheistic. Happily, some of them manage to work their way through Spong's writings and speeches to a much more robust version of the gospel. This is clearly by default, because Spong is headed towards a confused and half-hearted form of atheism. As we shall see when we turn later to look at the work of Donald Cupitt, his position is inherently unstable and quickly loses ground among its own initial devotees. Thus, we must conclude that those who look to Spong for help in renewal are likely to be deeply disappointed in the long run.

The issue needs to be pressed even harder. Spong's vision of renewal is profoundly destructive of the life of the church. In fact, the very existence of Spong as a bishop draws attention to a striking new feature of Christian existence that is very easily overlooked. We are clearly in the midst of a third schism in the church as a whole.[20] The first schism is that between East and West, the second is the schism between Protestant and Catholic, and the third is the schism between broadly orthodox and broadly post-orthodox forms of Christianity. It is very difficult to find the language to say what we need to say here neatly and non-pejoratively, but the point is clear: modern Christianity is now internally divided between those who, like Newbigin, are convinced that only some version of robust orthodoxy will work and those who, like Spong, are convinced that only a radically revisionist version of Christianity will work. This is a schism within and across denominations; it is not a schism out of, or away from, the existing denominations. Hence this form of division is both difficult to detect and easy to ignore. It has brought the ecumenical movement of the twentieth century to a standstill, and it is not likely to be resolved in the foreseeable future.

One reason for this is that the division no longer exists on the fringes of the church or in the isolated halls of the academy. It is now firmly lodged within the episcopate of the Western church as a whole and thus is expressed at the highest levels of leadership. Consequently, the church in the West can no longer rely on its bishops to preserve or even to care for the unity of the body. Some bishops, aided by thoroughly secular forms of election to office, have become representatives of various interest groups and caucuses. Far from teaching the faith or offering an attractive and persuasive exposition of its content, they make fun of it, protect

20. I owe this expression to personal conversation with Professor Andrew Walker.

those who undermine it, and use their considerable political skill to keep intelligent criticism at bay. Of course, in doing all this, they loudly proclaim their holy innocence and their virtue in making the faith credible in a new day. With a little effort they can even manage to cast themselves as a new class of victims deserving of our sympathy because of the attacks of self-righteous Fundamentalists. In these circumstances, those bishops who seek to preserve the catholic faith of the church are often dismissed as a right-wing party within the church as a whole. Not surprisingly, most bishops hide away in their work and do what they can to stand aloof from the fray that ensues. The overall result is obvious: the episcopate as a whole has become dysfunctional. It simply mirrors the nasty divisions now abroad in the church.

Laity, insofar as they are becoming aware of this, tend to adopt one of three strategies. First, disoriented and confused, they run from one local church or denomination to the next in the hopes of finding the Promised Land. Many take refuge in the closest version of congregationalism, not realizing that the faith there is no more secure than the faithfulness of the pastor and the board of elders. In short, the sheep wander on the hills in search of fresh pasture and are at risk from self-serving hirelings. Second, many organize and form vibrant renewal organizations in the hopes of changing the church from the bottom up. They become a small army in search of the enemy within. Inside these armies, roving investigative journalists attempt to keep the church as a whole informed of what is happening and readily develop the polemical and rhetorical skills to gain attention. The struggle for leadership within these groups can be otiose, and the cost of these operations can be astronomical. Given the worries that abound, there is no shortage of money. Worries about the money trail in turn lead to charges from some episcopal leaders and their friends that well-heeled, right-wing Fundamentalists are attempting to take over the mainline denominations. Ad hoc investigative committees that have the appearance but eschew the reality of objectivity are formed to name names. Thus there is a vicious circle of accusation and dissent that shows no signs of abating.

This naturally leads to a third option, namely, exiting the mainline Protestant tradition and finding security and solace in the Roman Catholic Church.[21] Here, away from the clash of parties and movements, believers hope that they can get relief from conflict and disagreement. Surely, they surmise, we can rely on Rome to protect us from the fury of Protestant dissent and disarray. Surely, they propose, we can find a vision of authority that will match the quest for an adequate theory of knowledge so eagerly sought by Newbigin and Spong. Surely, they think to themselves, we can find a true bishop and overseer of the faith and of our souls. So in one move they hope to be rid of the clash of interest groups, to find the right foundations for faith, and to find a true Father in the Faith. Maybe, they conclude, there is fresh hope for renewal after all. To that hope we turn in the chapter to follow.

---

21. Some, of course, turn to Eastern Orthodoxy. I shall take up the issue of renewal within that tradition in Chapter Six.

CHAPTER 4

TENSIONS IN ROME

ROSEMARY RADFORD RUETHER AND CARDINAL RATZINGER

IN OUR LAST CHAPTER WE SAW how two contrasting proposals on renewal emerged from the life experience of two distinguished bishops. Visions for renewal may also arise out of the experiences of groups of Christians. This is exactly the case with the two examples we shall explore in this chapter. In the first instance, we shall explore the work of Rosemary Radford Ruether (1936-), one of the leading theologians of contemporary feminism, and Cardinal Ratzinger (1927-), one of the leading interpreters and theologians of Vatican II, as they work out radically different responses to the aftermath of that remarkable council. We begin with Ruether because Cardinal Ratzinger's proposals are best seen in part as a response to the suggestions of feminists like Ruether. As we explore these options, we shall examine to what extent the hopes identified at the end of the last chapter may be realized by turning to Rome.

Ruether has been very intentional in thinking through and implementing a very particular vision of renewal. In fact, both early and late in her prolific career as a theologian, she stopped to take stock of her situation in two essays that provide an invaluable overview of her own efforts.[1] The two essays act as an illuminating set of bookends in a career that has established her as the leading feminist theologian of her genera-

---

1. Ruether, "The Free Church Movement in Contemporary Catholicism," Continuum, 6 (1968), 41-52; Ruether, "Church as Community," at http://www.corpus.org/archives/ruether_keynote.htm.

tion, and they show remarkable continuity in her thinking over thirty years.

Ruether takes her initial cue in renewal from the immediate failure of Vatican II. The hopes expressed by the council were indeed noble and attractive:

> In the euphoria which immediately followed after the second Vatican Council, it appeared that the Roman Catholic Church was actually accomplishing the near impossible; namely, an established institution renewing itself through the channels of constituted authority. It appeared that, after centuries of fear and stagnation, a revolutionary renewal was taking place that was to catapult the Roman Church into dialogue with modern times. There was to be a balanced assimilation of the best contemporary thought, but without loss of historical continuity, without schism or breaking of ranks on any side.[2]

As early as 1968, Ruether was skeptical of this possibility.

> It is one thing to define a noble theory of episcopal collegiality, we discover, quite another to put this into practice when it implies a concrete challenge to the old power structures and lines of authority which heretofore have prevailed. It is one thing to outline a beautiful concept of the church as a community and its liturgy as the celebration of its life together, but quite another to begin to scrutinize the present structure of the parish in the light of these ideas. In retrospect it becomes apparent that much of the image of unity and orderly self-renewal given by conciliar decrees was possible because these decrees sailed across the surface of the episcopal minds in an almost Platonic state of abstract discussion. But the liberal theologians who promoted these theories and sold them to the bishops did not fully anticipate and face up to the revolutionary implications of translating these theories into practice.[3]

---

2. Ruether, "Free Church Movement," p. 41.
3. Ruether, "Free Church Movement," p. 41.

The language of revolution is instructive. Ruether reads Vatican II as supplying an agenda for radical change within the Roman Catholic Church. The assumption in place is obvious: something has gone wrong in the institutional formation of the church. When Vatican II tried to fix this, a confrontation then emerged between two entirely different ways of thinking about Christianity, including

> The old mould of thought: formal, legal, triumphalist, defining all power as operating from the apex of the hierarchy down; this mould of thought is so far removed from the communal and secular orientation that characterizes modern Christian thought that the two points of view not only differ in their conclusions, but in their interpretation of practically all the premises as well.[4]

While conservatives and liberals may use the same symbols, they mean very different things by them. As they press their contrasting agendas, the result is not just a breakdown in communication but the emergence of schism: "We Catholics today may not yet have any formal institutional schism, but that is more an inherited cultural lag than an expression of inward unity. Spiritually we are already in schism."[5] At the top of the church there are the hierarchical power structures where lines of authority still proceed from the top down. Ranged against these structures are networks of bishops, priests, and laity, working to varying degrees underground, seeking to democratize the church from below. Because canonical theory provides no legitimacy for renewal from below, those involved in this revolutionary power struggle have to proceed as best they can:

> Therefore, they have to fall back on methods which border on sabotage, such as withholding funds, withdrawing from the parish and school, using the popular press to embarrass the hierarchy and to reveal its secret orders and decrees and, finally, massing together in un-

4. Ruether, "Free Church Movement," p. 42.
5. Ruether, "Free Church Movement," p. 43.

authorized organizations which can present a threat of sheer numbers to the hierarchy and which cannot be destroyed by individual reprisals.[6]

What emerges on the other side of these practices is a free church movement in Roman Catholicism. Catholics withdraw from hierarchical jurisdiction and set up their own para-insititutional organizations, communities, and forums by which their own voices might be heard.

We can begin to see the diagnosis that emerges from this analysis. Effectively, the Roman Catholic Church has become frozen in a network of institutional structures that are exclusionary in practice, juridical in orientation, and spiritually suffocating in effect. The church has ceased to function as community, operating as a top-down, hierarchical, bureaucratic body that stifles the work of the Holy Spirit in the church as a whole, but most especially among those whose voices have been ignored or silenced. Consequently, fresh insights arising from secular sources and more modern theological ways of thinking are stifled and suppressed. The chosen way out of this is the creation of free church structures that refuse a one-way, top-down mode of communication and authority.

Not surprisingly, given the conflict that ensues, renewalists differ in the kind of response they propose. Moderates generally want to work with the hierarchy, offering petitions, seeking permission for change, hoping for the integration of new possibilities into the current setup, and so on. They remain essentially church-directed. Radicals are much less patient, developing new organizations and communities that would replace the current structures once they are overthrown. They are less concerned about reform and updating and "more interested in being Christians than in being Roman Catholics, more interested in social witness than in churchmanship. . . ."[7]

All of the renewalists are vitally concerned about community at the local level, according to Ruether:

---

6. Ruether, "Free Church Movement," p. 44.
7. Ruether, "Free Church Movement," p. 45.

The present impersonal, territorial parishes are geared to an individualistic spirituality at best. They express no real community, either in
terms of shared decisions, meaningful action, or even a sense of real
joy and celebration together. They are drab, incredibly dull, insult-
ingly mediocre sacramental service stations, where people come to
fulfill some obligation and carry away as quickly as possible some
imaginary deposit of grace. Those who have a vision of the church as
a real Christian community in which communion with God is expressed in interpersonal concern, friendship, and joint action find the
typical parish untenable.[8]

Consequently, some renewalists take to doing church themselves
within the religious orders, across parish boundaries, in house churches,
in covenant groups, and in non-territorial parishes. Here they develop
their own liturgies and implement their own missionary strategies. In
some extreme cases the new group may break loose from the current
structures of the church. Thus, one group of liturgical radicals gave up on
the church as completely irrelevant and saw itself "as a floating spirit of
renewal abroad in the world" and saw the call of the Christian to assem-
ble as "essentially a call to go where the action is."[9]

The celebrants of such communities are charismatic. They arise as
the natural leadership of the group, and are designated, not by institutional authority, but by popular acclaim. They are the true gurus of
the community, and their authority can be acclaimed because it is a
charismatic authority which is created in and creates freedom, and
no longer has any connection to institutional subservience.[10]

Such *avante garde* groups have a crucial role overall in the spiritual economy of contemporary society: they meet the spiritual hunger for spiritual
experience that is a potent new force in the land but often cannot be met
by organized Christianity.

8. Ruether, "Free Church Movement," p. 47.
9. Ruether, "Free Church Movement," pp. 49-50.
10. Ruether, "Free Church Movement," pp. 49-50.

Ruether is committed to the democratization of the institutional church. Here the Free Church component is muted and restrained; the work of renewal would find

> . . . satisfactory completion at the point at which it succeeds in re-modeling the balance of power in the Roman Catholic Church along the lines which presently prevail in other modern denominations, such as the American Episcopal Church; i.e., when it achieves a situation in which the pastor is called to the parish through the co-operative effort of the bishop and an elected council of laymen who represent the congregation; when the parishes furnish elected lay as well as clerical representatives to make up a diocesan council which would have legislative powers as well as the power to elect the bishop; when a similar representative body with similar functions would also operate on the level of the national church and finally on the level of the international church, meeting in regular council to pass decrees and the power to elect the pope and to appoint working committees of the international church.[11]

This would not mean the end of hierarchy, but it would mean a decisive shift in the balance of power within the church.

For Ruether, however, this goal would only be a minimum first step. She has also prophesied and approved the emergence of a stronger version of the Free Church tradition. Now that the church, at least, in North America is disestablished, she looked forward to the recovery and continuation of "the free community within historical Christianity":[12]

> It is founded on a view of the church which denies that hierarchical institutionalization belongs to the essence of the church. The church is seen essentially as the gathered community of explicit believers in which sacramental distinctions between clergy and laity are abolished, priestly roles become purely contextual and functional; the

11. Ruether, "Free Church Movement," p. 51.
12. Ruether, "Free Church Movement," p. 51.

whole community arising by joint covenant entered into by the existential analogue of believer's baptism; that is to say, by voluntary adult decision. This concept of the believer's church is, I believe, the authentic church, and it is the understanding of the church which ever reappears in the avant garde at the moments of real church renewal. It is the avant garde and full expression of the church of renewal.[13]

So if in the first stage of renewal Roman Catholics are transposed into Anglicans, in the second they cease to be Anglicans and become Baptists.[14] They would, however, be Baptists with a difference, for Ruether has no desire in the end to replace the institutional church. At this point, she envisages a dialectical relation between the Free Church communities that would arise in renewal and the traditional institutional life of Roman Catholicism. The latter needs to remain, albeit as a secondary expression of the church:

The two are really interdependent polarities with the total dialectic of the church's existence. The charismatic community can be free to be itself when it can resign the work of transmission to the institution and allow itself to form its life and let go of its life only so long as the vital spirit lasts within it. The historical church, in turn, remains vital and is constantly renewed through its ability to take in and absorb the insights of the believer's church. But in order to receive the fruits of the believer's church, it must be willing to accept whatever freedom the believer's church feels is necessary for the flowering of its experimental spirits. It must be willing to let communities arise autonomously and without any specific kinds of institutional ties to work out their own gifts, and yet still remain in the kind of open communication with these free communities which will allow their fruits to

13. Ruether, "Free Church Movement," pp. 51-52.
14. We are working here with the analogical framework supplied by Ruether. In her career as a theologian, Ruether has developed a vision of systematic theology and of the womanchurch that is anything but Baptist in material content. See her *Sexism and God-Talk* (Boston: Beacon Press, 1983).

be given to the church as a whole. Only in this way does the whole dialectic of historical Christianity work as it should.[15]

If the church fails at this point, "the Holy Spirit flees outside the bounds of historical Christianity and takes up its work elsewhere."[16]

We might sum up Ruether's initial vision of renewal in this way. The late 1960s was a time of disillusionment within the Roman Catholic Church. The hopes engendered by Vatican II had not been realized. In reality, a hierarchical, self-serving institution had failed to follow through on its own commitments to renewal. The problem, then, was at once institutional, pastoral, and theological. Institutionally, the church was intransigent and ossified; pastorally, the church was boring and suffocating; theologically, the church had failed as community. The solution had to be equal parts institutional, pastoral, and theological. Institutionally, renewalists should form parachurch organizations, modeled to a lesser or greater degree on the Free Church tradition. Pastorally, the church needed to become a place of healing, friendship, and nurture. Theologically, renewalists should reconceive the church as community. Community constituted the primary form of the church; its institutional forms were secondary. Ideally, Christianity needed to be reorganized along dialectical lines, so that the institutional church could provide orderly transmission of the gospel and of the faith while charismatic communities supplied new insights, fresh creativity, and novel practices.

When Ruether returned to the topic in 1998, much of the vision developed thirty years earlier remained intact. In and around a fascinating review of her own life within the church, Ruether keeps alive most of the crucial ingredients of her original program. Thus, we find again a deep sense of alienation and frustration with the traditional structures of the Roman Catholic Church, the same commitment to democratic transformation, the same lament about local congregations as alienating and offensive, the same praise for the Free Church tradition as an alternative to the institutional church, the same drive towards community as practiced

15. Ruether, "Free Church Movement," pp. 51-52.
16. Ruether, "Free Church Movement," pp. 51-52.

in house churches, covenant communities, and the like, and the same dedication to a creative dialectic of chosen community and historical church. In addition, Ruether remains acutely aware that renewal movements themselves quickly become institutionalized; they thus run the same danger that emerged in the transition of the early church from community to institution. Exploring this shift to institutional structures provides a useful way of rounding off our exposition and of moving to a very different vision of renewal within the Roman Catholic tradition.

Ruether develops her vision of the fall of the church both historically and normatively. Historically, she makes the case in this fashion:

> The early church was primarily a charismatic community with little institutional apparatus. Leadership was drawn from those with recognized spiritual gifts of prophecy, healing and teaching. There was a certain breakdown of class, race, and gender hierarchies, as women and men, from both slave, freedman and artisan classes gathered across ethnic lines in cities like Corinth, Alexandria and Rome. It is this pattern of new relations, seen as manifesting a new order of redemption, that is expressed in the baptismal formula in Paul's letter to the Galatians, "In Christ no more Jew nor Greek, slave nor free, male and female."
>
> Gradually a hierarchical structure emerged, linking local congregations to a bishop in cities and then provinces of the empire, until the church began to approximate the bureaucratic system of the Roman empire, Rome and Constantinople. This bureaucratic structure made it easy for the emperors to incorporate Catholic Christianity into the bureaucracy of the empire as the state church in the fourth century. People began to join the church, not out of deep conviction, but because it was the politically advantageous and then necessary thing to do. Not to be a Catholic Christian was to be in trouble with the law.[17]

Ruether makes her case normatively as well:

17. Ruether, "Church as Community," p. 2.

The error of historical church institution lies in its efforts to make claims of spiritual efficacy for its purely institutional forms of mediation of words, symbols and rituals . . . in so doing, the institutional church creates a sacramental materialism that teaches people that only the actions of the validly ordained, according to its rubrics, can cause the gracious life of God to be present, and that they do this simply by the ritual acts, whether or not either the priest or the people interiorize this meaning. . . . The church thus creates a false faith in the spiritual power of material acts. It asserts that spiritual power is available because the historical church stands in legitimate succession of transmission through episcopal succession that goes back to the apostles ordained by Christ, and so it alone is the church founded by Christ. This legitimizing myth of apostolic succession needs to be re-examined. It is historically false that Jesus founded or intended to found such a historical church with a hierarchical government based on the model of the Roman empire. . . . The institutional church of episcopal hierarchy is not the successor of this apostolic church; it arose by suppressing this apostolic church.[18]

We can begin our exposition of Cardinal Ratzinger's proposals on the renewal of the church at exactly this juncture. For Ratzinger the crisis facing the modern church is a "crisis of ecclesial consciousness."[19] If this crisis is to be resolved, we need to "find the patience first to ask about her nature, her origin, her destination. . . ."[20] Hence Ratzinger, like Ruether, considers it imperative to work through to a vision of the church in her origination and development across space and time. Thereafter they diverge, providing radically different interpretations of the relevant data. For Ratzinger, Ruether's vision represents in part what is at fault in the modern church, namely, a set of dualisms: between spirit and body, priest and prophet, charism and institution, laity and hierarchy, and the like. A proper vision of the church will find a way beyond these contrasts.

18. Ruether, "Church as Community," p. 5.

19. Joseph Cardinal Ratzinger, *Called to Communion: Understanding the Church Today* (San Francisco: Ignatius, 1996), p. 11.

20. Ratzinger, *Called to Communion*, p. 9.

Ratzinger is well aware that mapping a historical account of the origins of the church is a contested enterprise. Historical investigation of the church is not a neutral theological practice; it is an engaged activity where our own theological commitments play a critical role. As a result, the quest for the historical Jesus and the historical church has become "so overgrown by the tangled thicket of exegetical hypothesis that there is seemingly next to no hope of finding any sort of adequate answer to it."[21] A century of study has made this all too clear. Historical study of Jesus and of the church focused a hundred years ago on Jesus as the great individualist who liberated religion from cultic institutions, reduced religion to ethics, and grounded everything on the individual conscience. Clearly, on pain of inconsistency, this Liberal Jesus cannot found a church. In sharp reaction against this, the historical work between World War I and World War II rediscovered the church. The ecumenical consensus that arose and stretched from Moscow to Washington is staggering in its simplicity. Understanding worship became integral to understanding the Old Testament and Jesus. In particular, Jesus came to be seen as founding a new community by means of the Lord's Supper; in turn, the Lord's Supper became the rule of the church's life.

This consensus collapsed after World War II, and scholars returned to a more liberal vision of origins. Reflecting wider cultural splits between East and West, neoliberal and Marxist, and First and Third World, scholars seized on Jesus as an eschatological prophet and resurrected the old contrasts between priest and prophet. Thus cult, institution, and law were pitted against prophecy, charism, and creative freedom. Jesus, as the prophet of the End, proclaimed the end of institutions. The message of Jesus lives on as a revolutionary breakthrough from the institutional realm into the charismatic realm, where the church ceaselessly recreates its own forms. In Marxist-oriented circles, the opposition between priest and prophet became a cipher for the class struggle. Jesus became a symbol of the oppressed proletariat; the eschatological message became a message of the end of the class-society; and the priest-prophet dialectic

21. Ratzinger, *Called to Communion*, p. 14.

expressed the dynamics of history on its way to the classless society. According to Ratzinger,

> Ecclesiology now becomes newly significant: it is fitted into the dialectical framework already set up by the division into priests and prophets, which is conflated with a corresponding distinction between institution and people. In accordance with this dialectical model, the "popular Church" is pitted against the institutional or "official Church." This "popular Church" is ceaselessly born out of the people and in this way carries forward Jesus' cause: his struggle against institutions and their oppressive power for the sake of a new and free society that will be the "Kingdom."[22]

Given such disagreement, it is tempting to opt for the most congenial historical option on offer or to become skeptical of the whole enterprise. Ratzinger's strategy tries to avoid both temptations. He suggests we factor out obvious ideological contamination, and that we work from the basic memory of the church. In essence he transposes the consensus of the mid-War period.[23] His vision of the church runs something like this. Jesus of Nazareth both proclaimed the arrival of the kingdom of God and gathered together the people of God. "The kingdom was promised, what came was Jesus."[24] Yet Jesus was and is never alone. He gathered what was dispersed. In drawing people to God, he exposed the dynamic of unification: as we move toward God, we are drawn together as one. Equally, Jesus displayed the point of convergence: we become a people solely through his call and our response to his call and to his person. Thus Jesus called his followers into a new family and gave them a rule of prayer. He had a compactly knit core of twelve disciples, representing the tribes of Israel, flanked by seventy or seventy-two, representing the number of non-Jewish peoples of the world. Within this com-

---

22. Ratzinger, *Called to Communion*, pp. 18-19.

23. It would take us off track here to chase down how successful this move is epistemologically.

24. Ratzinger, *Called to Communion*, p. 23. Ratzinger here cleverly inverts Loisy's famous aphorism: "The Kingdom was promised; what came was the church."

munity, he instituted, in analogy with Passover and the Sinaitic covenant ritual, a new meal, the Eucharist, that became the bond uniting a new people of God. This Eucharist is the permanent origin and center of the church, joining the diverse peoples of the world to the one Lord and to his one and only Body.

This vision of the church was carried over into the church's understanding of itself. Thus the church intentionally identified itself as the "assembly of the people," which, like the assembly of Israel, listened to what God proclaimed and assented to it. Gathered around the crucified and risen Christ, those joined to him were the final gathering of God's people. This gathering was not a natural event; it emanated from Christ and is sustained by the Holy Spirit. It was centered in the Lord, who joins us with himself and with each other in baptism and who communicates himself in his very Body and Blood. Equally, to shift to a Pauline analogy, the church saw itself as the body of Christ. This hackneyed image was no mere borrowing from Stoic philosophy. It carried rich biblical overtones: it transmitted the Old Testament sense of being a corporate personality, where the walls between individuals disappear, so that "I" and "Thou" mutually interpenetrate. Further, it carried Eucharistic overtones, with Christ's followers assimilated to Jesus and to each other in the one "bread" and thus made one body. Finally, it furnished nuptial overtones in which Christ's disciples become one flesh in a spiritual-bodily union that erodes the infidelity of self-willed autonomy.

The very same vision of the church, represented by the notions of "assembly" and "body of Christ," is clearly on display, argues Ratzinger, in the early chapters of Luke's narrative ecclesiology in Acts. Thus, the disciples and Mary met as an "assembly of the people." It was not a parliament, but a community of prayer, numbering exactly 120 to signify both its connection to the Twelve and to its worldwide future. Moreover, the community adhered to the teaching and fellowship of the apostles, to the breaking of bread, and to the prayers. In between stood Pentecost. Hence the church was not the decision of human agents; she was the creature of the wind and fire of the Holy Spirit, who is love. The Holy Spirit at once banished uniformity, domination, subjection, hatred, and division, and fostered interplay of plurality and unity across linguistic and ethnic identities. From this analysis, we can see that from the beginning, the church was a world church. As Ratzinger put it,

> Luke thus rules out a conception in which a local Church first arose in Jerusalem and then became the base for the gradual establishment of other local Churches that eventually grew into a federation. Luke tells us that the reverse is true: what first exists is the one Church, the Church that speaks in all tongues — the *ecclesia universalis;* she then generates Church in the most diverse locales, which are nonetheless always the embodiment of the one and only Church. The temporal and ontological priority lies with the universal Church; a Church that was not Catholic would not even have ecclesial reality.[25]

There is one dramatic note to add to Ratzinger's use of Luke:

> In order to express the catholicity of the Church created by the Holy Spirit, he [Luke] has made use of an old, presumably Hellenistic scheme of twelve peoples. This scheme is closely related to the lists of nations compiled in the states that succeeded the empire of Alexander. Luke enumerates these twelve peoples and their languages as receivers of the apostolic word, yet at the end he breaks out of its scheme by adding a thirteenth people: the Romans.[26]

This editorial amendment is no accident on Luke's part; for Ratzinger, it is a critical theological statement that makes Rome both the capitulation of the pagan world and a constitutive dimension of catholicity:

> Paul's arrival in Rome marks the goal of the path that began in Jerusalem; the universal — the catholic — Church has been realized, in continuance of the ancient chosen people and its history and taking over the latter's mission. Thus Rome, as a symbol for the world of nations, has a theological status in Acts; it cannot be separated from the Lukan idea of catholicity.[27]

25. Ratzinger, *Called to Communion,* p. 44.
26. Ratzinger, *Called to Communion,* p. 44.
27. Ratzinger, *Called to Communion,* p. 45.

This final move to incorporate Rome into the very idea of Catholicity is unnervingly elegant and brilliant. With a simple appeal to Acts, Ratzinger has found a foothold for the primacy of Peter and the unity of the Church. The next phase of the vision exploits this foothold to defend a robustly Roman Catholic vision of the church as indispensable to renewal today.

At this point Ratzinger makes a case in a fresh and succinct way for the primacy of Peter among the Twelve and in the early tradition, for the principle of succession in general, and for the reality of Petrine succession in Rome. The crucial elements in the argument can be summarized in a bundle of propositions. 1. Peter was the first witness of the resurrection; thereby he was installed as of first rank among the apostles. 2. Paul submitted his message for evaluation to Peter as one of the three "pillars" of the church in Jerusalem, thus recognizing communion with the pillars as the criterion of possessing the one common gospel. Given that the other pillars, James and John, dropped from prominence, "the fact stands that every preaching of the gospel must gauge itself by the preaching of Peter."[28] In their own way, the gospels of John and Luke confirm the early and pervasive primacy of Peter. 3. Peter enjoyed a special position in the circle of the Twelve. Thus Peter was the spokesman at the Transfiguration; and he was the one addressed in the Lord's hour of anguish in the Garden of Olives. He was given a new name, "Rock," by Jesus, a designation that betokened a special place in the struggle against chaos and destruction. He became "the rock that stands against the impure tide of unbelief and its destruction of man."[29] 4. Christ's commission of Peter in Matthew 16:17-19 fit perfectly with these background proposals. Peter confessed Christ by the revelation of the Father. He received the promise that the gates of hell would not prevail against him, a promise "for the time-transcending gathering of the new people."[30] He received the power of the keys. He was now the doorkeeper, who had to judge concerning

28. Ratzinger, *Called to Communion*, p. 52.
29. Ratzinger, *Called to Communion*, p. 56.
30. Ratzinger, *Called to Communion*, p. 63. Initially agreement with Antioch, Rome, and Alexandria was essential. However, as Ratzinger sees it, Peter lies behind all three sees, Antioch and Rome directly, Alexandria indirectly through Mark.

admission and rejection. Equally, he had the power of binding and loosing, so that he could make doctrinal decisions, administer discipline, and deliver the word of divine forgiveness. 5. There was a succession of structure, which went beyond succession in word and witness, and which passed from Peter across the generations. From the beginning, the presence of Christ and the Holy Spirit was sacramentally transmitted through word and person by the laying on of hands. 6. Against the Gnostic threat, this succession was given fixed reference points within the apostolic sees. Within these sees there was "a decisive criterion that recapitulates all others: the church at Rome, where Peter and Paul suffered martyrdom. It was with this Church that every community had to agree: Rome was the standard of the authentic apostolic tradition as a whole."[31] This criterion of the right apostolic faith was older than the canon of the New Testament; indeed, Rome was one of the internal and external conditions of the possibility of the New Testament as Bible.

The upshot of these reflections is pivotal for Ratzinger's vision. The Roman primacy is an essential element of ecclesial unity. This has nothing to do with human schemes of dominion; nor is it undermined by sin and failure in the papal office. Roman primacy is a gift of God, made possible and sustained by God:

> Every single biblical logion about the primacy thus remains from generation to generation a signpost and a norm, to which we must ceaselessly resubmit ourselves. When the Church adheres to these words in faith, she is not being triumphalistic but humbly recognizing in wonder and thanksgiving the victory of God over and through human weakness. Whoever deprives these words of their force for fear of triumphalism or of human usurpation of power does not proclaim that God is greater but diminishes him, since God demonstrates the power of his love, and thus remains faithful to the law of the history of salvation, precisely in the power of human impotence. For with the same realism with which we today declare the sins of the popes and their disproportion to the magnitude of their commission,

31. Ratzinger, *Called to Communion*, p. 69.

we must also acknowledge that Peter has stood as the rock against all ideologies, against the dissolution of the word into the plausibilities of a given time, against subjection to the powers of this world.[32]

While the actual logistics and the detailed mode of the exercise of papal primacy in and through the local bishops is a matter of the highest importance, the crux of the issue is that the papal office is integral to the unity and catholicity of the church.[33] Thus the Orthodox claim that the local Eucharistic celebration is enough to constitute the church is radically incomplete, because, as the Orthodox themselves agree, there is no Eucharist without the bishop. The bishop serves the communion of the faithful by linking the local church to the whole church. The Protestant tendency towards a congregationalism that rests content with the preaching of the Word and the presence of the risen Lord among the two or three gathered in his name is equally insufficient; in such a vision, the "catholicity of the church crumbles away."[34] The Church is the Eucharist; the Church is communion. But this communion is never with Jesus alone but with One who has given himself a Body. Thus communion with Jesus is catholic or it is nothing. However, to be catholic, the local church must be linked with the whole people of God through space and time. Hence it must be connected to those divinely given structures that serve the ends of unity with God and unity with each other. Within these structures, the bishop of Rome has always had a privileged position. Indeed,

> the juridical expression of unity in the office of Peter's successor and in the necessary dependence of the bishops both on one another and on him belongs to the core of her sacred order. Hence the loss of this element wounds her at the point where she is most truly church.[35]

---

32. Ratzinger, *Called to Communion,* pp. 73-74.

33. "This will remain, the magisterial responsibility for the unity of the Church, her faith, and her morals that was defined by Vatican I and II." See Ratzinger, *Salt of the Earth: Christianity and the Catholic Church at the End of the Millennium* (San Francisco: Ignatius, 1997), p. 257.

34. Ratzinger, *Called to Communion,* p. 82.

35. Ratzinger, *Called to Communion,* p. 94.

It is now relatively easy to anticipate Ratzinger's diagnosis of the present ills of the church. His deepest and persistent worry is that the church faces undermining from within by groups who seek to destabilize her catholicity. The issue is not first and foremost papal primacy; papal primacy comes, so to speak, with the total package. The bigger issue is the integrity of the church as a Eucharistic, public, catholic community designed by the Triune God. Clearly the threat to stability comes from the impulse to overturn the divinely ordained structures of the church. The obvious way to do this is to press for democratic or ideologically driven interpretations of the Christian faith as substitutes for the real thing. The problem is indeed "a crisis of ecclesial consciousness."

We might also describe the problem as one of accommodation to the impulses of modernity.[36] Thus the church's legitimate consciousness is challenged initially in the name of freedom. The limits set by the church are irksome and burdensome. As Ratzinger put it,

> They inwardly affect my course in life telling me how I am supposed to understand and shape my freedom. They demand of me decisions that cannot be made without painful renunciation. Is this not intended to deny us the sweetest fruits in the garden of life? Is not the way into the wide open closed by the restrictive confines of so many commandments and prohibitions? Is not thought kept from reaching its full stature just as much as the will is? Must not liberation consist in breaking out of such immature dependency? And would not the only real reform be to rid ourselves of the whole business?[37]

Those standing in the way of this liberation are dismissed as reactionaries and Fundamentalists. The church must be turned into a democracy, integrating into her constitution the basic patrimony of rights and freedoms elaborated by the European Enlightenment.

---

36. Ratzinger can also state the accommodation in terms of yielding to power politics in the name of oppression. See Ratzinger, *Salt of the Earth*, pp. 165-66. Both versions of freedom, the personal and the political, clearly stem from versions of the Enlightenment.

37. Ratzinger, *Called to Communion*, pp. 134-35.

We must move — it is maintained — from the paternalistic Church to the Community Church; no one must any longer remain a passive receiver of the gift of Christian existence. Rather, all should be active agents of it. The Church must no longer be fitted over from above like a ready-made garment; no, we "make" the Church ourselves, and do so in constantly new ways. It thus finally becomes "our" Church, for which we make ourselves actively responsible. The Church arises out of discussion, compromise and resolution. Debate brings out what can still be asked of people today, which can still be considered by common consent as faith or ethical norms. New formulas of faith are composed.[38]

Concomitantly, new liturgies are composed. Scripture is selectively mined for material that will provide self-realization. Democratic self-determination becomes the order of the day. Minorities must submit to majorities who possess no infallible guarantee of representing the wishes of those who elect them and whose decisions can in time be revoked by another majority. The end is disastrous:

A church based on human resolutions becomes a merely human church. It is reduced to the level of the makeable, of the obvious, of opinion. Opinion replaces faith. And in fact, in the self-made formulas of faith with which I am acquainted, the meaning of the words "I believe" never signifies anything beyond "we opine." Ultimately the self-made church savors of the "self," which always has a bitter taste to the other self and just as soon reveals its petty insignificance. A self-made church is reduced to the empirical domain and thus, precisely as a dream, comes to nothing.[39]

True renewal takes a different path. It allows the true form of the church given by God to be constantly renewed across the generations.

---

38. Ratzinger, *Called to Communion*, p. 137.
39. Ratzinger, *Called to Communion*, pp. 139-40.

The fundamental liberation that the Church can give us is to permit us to stand in the horizon of the eternal and to break out of the limits of our knowledge and our capacities. In every age, therefore, the faith itself in its full magnitude and breadth is the essential reform that we need; it is in the light of faith that we must test the value of self-constructed organizations in the Church.[40]

For Ratzinger, faith does not hang in mid-air, flitting around without content and structure. It is centered in Jesus Christ, who handed over the keys to Peter and thereby transmitted the authority to let in, to bring home, and to forgive. Such forgiveness, in turn, is not merely some abstract, juridical phenomenon. Forgiveness is "an active-passive event: the creative word of power that God speaks to us produces the pain of conversion and thus becomes an active self-transformation."[41] Moreover, obscuration of the grace of forgiveness is at the basis of the spiritual crisis of our time. We may indeed applaud the fact that morality is coming back into favor. However, where forgiveness guaranteed by authority is not recognized or believed, we are left with a fog of discussions in which guilt evaporates. This way of removing guilt is too cheap; those truly liberated know that there is sin and that there must be a real way to overcome it. This forgiveness bespeaks the need for atonement and expiation, so that morality, forgiveness, and expiation form an unbroken circle. Moreover, because forgiveness touches the very core of a person, "it gathers men together and is also the center of the renewal of community."[42] Within that community, we are connected not just with local activists, or with the crowd that meets to celebrate the Eucharist, or even with the pope, bishops, and priests, but with all the saints across the ages. It is not enough to have fortuitous majorities to decide our path; the saints become the normative majority by which we orient ourselves. In turn we move beyond simply *fighting* against suffering; we readily *rejoice* in our

---

40. Ratzinger, *Called to Communion*, p. 145. Ratzinger finds analogies between our current situation and the crises precipitated by the Gnostics and by Arius. See Ratzinger, *Salt of the Earth*, p. 162.

41. Ratzinger, *Called to Communion*, p. 149

42. Ratzinger, *Called to Communion*, p. 153.

sufferings, so that we may complete in our flesh "what is still lacking in the afflictions of Christ for the sake of his body, the Church" (Col. 1:24).[43] In the end, the choice is simple: we can become members of a party for Christ, or we can become members of the living church; we can opt for our own ideologies, or we can take our stand with the church across the ages.

The irony of the situation is that it is Ratzinger who is labeled the ideologue, at least in the popular image of his more recent work.[44] Prior to his rise to prominence within the Vatican hierarchy as the Prefect for the Congregation for the Doctrine of the Faith, Ratzinger was lauded as a progressive.[45] In his rise to favor within the academy, he had come close to failing his doctoral degree because he challenged the prevailing orthodoxy in theology.[46] He played a critical role in ensuring that Vatican II would openly tackle issues of substance rather than act as a rubber stamp for documents prepared in advance by the Roman curia.[47] Moreover, he provided lively and very intelligent commentaries on the work of the Council as a whole. Thus some have seen his later work as a betrayal both of his progressive promise and of Vatican II. There is, however, a much more generous and more accurate way to read Ratzinger's journey.

In keeping with Vatican II, Ratzinger initially saw the renewal of the church as intimately related to a dialectical tension within the life of the church. On the one hand there was a need to reach back to the Scriptures and to the Fathers so as to provide adequate resources for today. This

---

43. Ratzinger, *Called to Communion*, p. 155.

44. Compare the comment of Allen: "Ratzinger's critics often portray him as a man driven by fear — of losing power, of women, of sex, of modernity." See John L. Allen, Jr., *Cardinal Ratzinger: The Vatican's Enforcer of the Faith* (New York: Continuum, 2000), p. 310. See also Peter Seewald: "It is commonly conjectured that there are two Ratzingers: one before Rome, a progressive, and the other in Rome, the conservative and stern guardian of the faith. So the former theological teenager with progressive traits becomes a resigned conservative with occasional apocalyptic moods" (*Salt of the Earth*, p. 115). In some circles Ratzinger has been referred to as the *Panzerkardinal*. See *Salt of the Earth*, p. 84.

45. The task of the Congregation is to protect sound doctrine, to correct errors, and to lead the erring back to the right path.

46. See Ratzinger, *Milestones: Memoirs, 1927-77* (San Francisco: Ignatius, 1997), pp. 107-9. One of Ratzinger's examiners was worried about a dangerous modernism in his work.

47. Ratzinger achieved this by writing a sensational speech for Bishop Frings of Cologne. See *Salt of the Earth*, p. 71.

ressourcement provided new vigor for the internal renewal of the church in liturgy, preaching, theological method, Scripture study, spirituality, and the like. On the other hand, the church needed to engage with the world as it is in all its doubt, suffering, material poverty, and oppression. This *aggiornamento* would be intrinsically required as an act of obedience to the Lord of history and creation; it would also prevent the retrieval of the patristic resources from becoming a narcissistic end in itself.[48] Ratzinger was clear that both were critical for genuine renewal. What happened, however, was that engagement with the world tended to undercut the retrieval of past treasures. Engagement took on a life of its own; in many instances it was transposed into ideology. Hence, renewal required a course correction. The reassertion of papal primacy, and the exercise of moral and doctrinal discipline that went with it, were therefore absolutely essential. They were not a lapse into a neo-conservative ideology. Moreover, they were entirely in line with Ratzinger's early scholarly retrieval of the vision of human nature he found in his studies of Augustine and Bonaventure. Thus we can provide a generous reading of Ratzinger that eschews reaching for flaws in character as determinative of his proposals on renewal.

Standing back for a moment and reviewing the twin proposals under review, we can now take up the queries posed at the end of the last chapter and repeated at the outset of this one. How far can we escape the weal and woe of contemporary mainline divisions by turning to renewal in the Roman Catholic tradition? How far can Rome help in dealing with the quest for an adequate vision of knowledge that has been such a marked feature of church life in the West? Clearly, if there are problems on either front, the spiritual solace so many have hoped for in Rome may prove to be illusory.

One thing is immediately clear. The rift within Protestantism represented by Bishop Lesslie Newbigin and Bishop John Shelby Spong emerges afresh in the obvious contrasts between Ruether and Ratzinger. Ruether acknowledges this when she speaks of a schism within the bor-

---

48. The importance of this point is well brought out by Aidan Nichols, OP, *The Theology of Joseph Ratzinger: An Introductory Study* (Edinburgh: T&T Clark, 1988), pp. 97-98.

ders of contemporary Catholicism. This is a sobering and accurate observation. So, it is now the case that within both Protestantism and Roman Catholicism, some visions of renewal expose and deepen schism rather than heal it. The quest for a radical and revisionist vision of the Christian faith is every bit as vibrant within Roman Catholicism as it is within mainline Protestantism. We may have escaped the old frying pan, but we have not escaped the fire.

We can resolve this, of course, by rejecting Ruether and embracing the vision of Ratzinger, but there is a high price to pay for such a move. This takes us to a second point. There is no simple way to resolve the competing historical visions of the origins and development of the church that are at the core of the differences between Ruether and Ratzinger. Ratzinger tries to transcend the differences by siphoning out ideologically contaminated material and by trusting in the memory of the church. However, there is no access to the memory of the church that does not itself depend on historical judgment, which is exactly the point at issue in the debate. Moreover, at a critical point in his historical reconstruction, that is, at the authenticity of the famous Matthean text on the power of the keys (Matt. 16:17-19), Ratzinger abandons historical investigation altogether:

> A saying of Jesus reported in the Bible is not made binding on faith because it is acknowledged as Jesus' word by the majority of contemporary exegetes, and it does not lose its validity when the opposite is the case. It is valid because Holy Scripture is valid and because Scripture presents it to us as an utterance of Jesus. Said in other terms: the guarantee of its validity does not result from hypothetical constructs, however well founded they might be, but from inclusion in the canon of Scripture, which in turn the faith of the Church avouches as the Word of God, that is, as the trustworthy ground of existence.[49]

In other words, the words of Jesus in Scripture are used to validate the authority of the church, and the authority of the church is then used to

49. Ratzinger, *Called to Communion*, pp. 58-59.

validate the authority of Scripture. We need not press the circularity of this argument. Nor need we challenge at this point the tendentious and selective reading of Scripture and church history that are patent in Ratzinger's arguments.[50] What is pertinent is the quick impasse that emerges when we appeal to the historical Jesus and the historical church. In turn, this impasse very quickly passes into a more general impasse about authority. We have rival visions of Jesus and of the church riding on the backs of rival theories of knowledge.

I do not think we can avoid this impasse, and I shall sally forth at the end with my own reading of the history. But we should have no illusions. Charges and countercharges of ideology are simply inescapable at this point. The dilemma that ensues is obvious. If renewal depends on resolving the problem of authority and thus getting the epistemology straight, Ratzinger has landed us right back where we were with Draper, Newbigin, and Spong. We are floundering in a sea of rival theories of warrant that keep us going round in circles. The appeal to Petrine primacy and papal infallibility does not solve the problem; it simply puts epistemology right back on the table. Worse still, it puts epistemology into the very heart of the faith. The bishop of Rome, once a revered and crucial bishop in the church as a whole, has been turned into an epistemic mechanism for securing the right interpretation of the gospel. Papal infallibility is integral to the understanding and survival of the faith. This is surely epistemology with a vengeance.

For Ruether, the primary problem is not initially epistemological. For her the deep issue is the evils that befall the institutional life of the church. While she insists that the problems we face are also theological and pastoral, clearly some of her most intimate concerns are political and sociological in nature. Hence her solution is a call for genuine community as exemplified in the Free Church tradition. This surely provides a different angle of vision on renewal. Yet it is embedded in a wider perspective that is every bit as tied to a liberal Protestant agenda in epistemology as is the vision offered by Spong. For Ruether, the ultimate foundation of the Christian faith is religious experience. The difference in her

---

50. To take the first obvious example, Peter is not the first witness of the resurrection.

case from the standard version of this theory of authority is that she simply extends the appeal to religious experience to give a privileged position to women's experience. As I have argued elsewhere, that is a very precarious exercise.[51]

There is an additional problem in Ruether. There is a deep tension, if not insuperable contradiction, at the core of her work. She would really like the Roman Catholic Church to transform itself into a modern mainline Protestant denomination. From even the most minimal Catholic angle, this is simply impossible. The Roman Catholic Church has looked at that option since the days of the Reformation and very understandably turned it down. Ruether, in her own inimitable way, acknowledges that her proposal is a pipedream. Yet she sticks with it because she knows that institutions are inescapable, and because she wants a version of Free Church Protestantism that can still benefit from the resources mediated through the long-standing institutions of the church across the ages. The challenge to the renewalism that emerges out of this is simple: can we have a vision of renewal that avoids the chaotic, self-destructive tendencies of the Free Church tradition and yet that also avoids the epistemological requirements that Ratzinger would impose on us?

Much as we might crave a resolution of the challenge just enunciated, we need to turn away from the obsession with theories of knowledge and take for a time a different route towards renewal. At this stage we are coming to the midpoint of our reflections, so it is time for a respite. Moreover, it would be good to be able to register even a modest measure of success. With that in mind we turn to the moral renovation of the tradition.

---

51. See William J. Abraham, *Canon and Criterion in Christian Theology* (Oxford: Clarendon, 1998), pp. 440-44.

CHAPTER 5

DYING FOR RENEWAL

MARTIN LUTHER KING JR. AND ARCHBISHOP ROMERO

PROPOSALS ABOUT THE RENEWAL of the church need not grow by some strict law of intention followed by action. Some proposals arise more spontaneously, developing from a network of experiences that create their own momentum and themes. Equally, proposals about renewal can easily be missed because they come to be interpreted in purely secular forms. Even though they clearly involve description, diagnosis, and prescription for the life of the church, these ingredients can remain tacit, as the process of renewal itself takes on a whole life of its own.

Nowhere are these developments more visible than in the life and work of Martin Luther King Jr. (1929-1968) and of Archbishop Oscar Romero (1917-1980). In these instances, the move to the renewal of the church catches the chief agents of renewal off guard; and the shape of renewal becomes such that it flourishes above and beyond its initial ecclesiastical home.

This should not surprise us in the least, for two reasons. First, schemes of renewal often reflect a particular diagnosis in which cultural, political, and other factors play a crucial role. The problems of the church are seen as integrally related to problems in the culture at large, and vice versa. Second, given the nature of the Christian gospel, the impact of the gospel on the world at large is a matter of decisive significance. The renewal of the gospel will always have serious consequences for society, which is one reason why revival and renewal are often feared by secularists, pluralists, or established religious confessionalists. Some become paranoid about renewal, worried that it will radically disrupt good order. These fears are far from groundless.

As we proceed to unpack the proposals that lie in and around the life of Martin Luther King Jr. it is crucial to note their importance for the broader discussion. Much popular thinking about renewal has great difficulty seeing that King belongs in the discussion. Renewal is often cast in purely pious or ecclesiastical terms; in some circles, it is limited to the restoration of personal piety. Yet earlier forms of renewal were robustly social and even political in their orientation. Thus the Puritans were extremely interested in the political dimensions of their efforts; John Wesley was intent on reforming not just the church but also the nation. Hence in turning to King we are not introducing alien elements into the debate. We are restoring a component that may well be pivotal for a proper handling of our subject. Renewal is not just private and personal, nor can it be confined to the life of the church. So we need to know the place moral and political action may have in renewal both conceptually and historically. King's life and work raise these issues dramatically.

King stumbled into renewal by accident. Certainly he never set out to fix either the church or the world according to some predetermined vision. In his words,

> . . . although we had come back to the South with the hope of playing a part in the changes we knew were on the horizon, we had no notion yet of how the changes would come about, and no inkling that in a little more than a year we would be involved in a movement that was to alter Montgomery forever and to have repercussions throughout the world.[1]

For the most part King was feeling his way; the central themes he developed were as much part of his own personal pilgrimage as they were

---

1. James M. Washington, ed., *A Testament of Hope: The Essential Writings and Speeches of Martin Luther King, Jr.* (San Francisco: HarperCollins, 1991), p. 423.

extraordinary public events. The resources he inherited and reworked in his ministry were manifold and eclectic. Brought up in a relatively prosperous African American world, he was early on immersed in the revivalism that was such a marked feature of the tradition he inherited. He was baptized at the age of five, a move prompted by the desire to keep abreast of his older sister. By the age of twelve he was airing doubts about the bodily resurrection of Jesus in Sunday school. Brilliant in high school, he went off to Morehouse College at the age of fifteen, having already displayed extraordinary rhetorical and oratorical skills. Academically he was interested in sociology as an undergraduate, but his intellectual formation really took off when he was a student at seminary. At Crozier Theological Seminary he read voraciously, developing a keen interest in theology and philosophy.[2] From there he went to Boston University for his doctorate. Over time he abandoned the Fundamentalism of his father, readily embraced the central elements of the liberal Protestantism of his best teachers, and went on to wrestle with the robust doctrine of sin reintroduced into American mainstream Christianity by Reinhold Niebuhr. Clearly, concern about social ethics was never far below the surface of his thinking. From the outset, both in his oratory and in his thinking, while he loved to work at and from the particularity of lived experience, he constantly scanned the world of ideas in order to find an appropriate intellectual horizon within which to lodge his practical proposals. The practical and the intellectual were then fused in a torrent of brilliant rhetoric and oratory that could be electrifying in its effect. One journalist described the impact of one of King's speeches as nothing less than "a Damascus road experience."[3]

Given this extraordinary network of gifts, it is not surprising that King chose the pastorate over the academy as the path to follow. One can well imagine King spending his life climbing up the ladder of homiletical brilliance, riding out a ministry that would end in happy retirement and ease. Rosa Parks's refusal to yield her bus seat to a white man in Mont-

---

2. King carried this learning with him into his sermons, constantly buttressing his theological moves with appeals to figures like Heraclitus, Hegel, Kant, Thoreau, Carlyle, Whitehead, and Eliot, to name only a few.

3. Michael Frady, *Martin Luther King, Jr.* (New York: Viking, 2002), p. 3.

gomery, Alabama, on December 1, 1955, shattered this cozy trajectory. Drawn into the fray by other pastors, King found himself at the center of a civil rights movement that changed him forever and eventually cost him his life. We need not trace King's journey from Montgomery, through Albany, Birmingham, Washington, and Selma, to his tragic murder. What is of interest here is his interpretation of the situation within and without the church, his vision of what had gone wrong, and his proposals for a way forward.

King begins with the harsh reality of moral and political evil, but not for one moment does he leave us there. Whatever the evolution in his thinking may have been, clear lines of description, diagnosis, and prescription emerge over time. These lines undermine any neat demarcation of the eternal from the moral, the cultural, the social, and the political. As we shall see, King begins with mundane realities like bus rides and voting in the South, but he ends with a vision that stretches across international space into eternity. He begins his prescription with the awakening of the black church, but he ends with a revolution that is meant to change not just the church but also the whole world.

The initial problem for King was racial segregation. Across the South, segregation was manifest in a host of ways: in buses, in restaurants, in housing areas, in schools, in trains, and in churches. Blacks were kept separate from whites by law, custom, convention, morality, and religion. In and around this world that stretched from law to religion, there swirled another world of bigotry, hatred, prejudice, poverty, and violence. All sides within the church appeared to have made their peace with this arrangement. Even those unhappy with the prevailing bargain were sufficiently driven by the desire for good order to leave things as they were. Hence the church, which should have become part of the solution, was itself part of the problem.

King expressed his worries graphically in his famous Letter from Birmingham Jail:

> I have traveled the length and breadth of Alabama, Mississippi and all the other southern states. On sweltering summer days and crisp autumn mornings I have looked at her beautiful churches with their

lofty spires pointing heavenward. I have beheld the impressive outlay of her massive religious education buildings. Over and over again I have found myself asking: "What kind of people worship here? Who is their God? Where were their voices when the lips of Governor Barnett dripped with words of interposition and nullification? Where were they when Governor Wallace gave the clarion call for defiance and hatred? Where were their voices of support when tired, bruised and weary Negro men and women decided to rise from the dark dungeons of complacency to the bright hills of creative protest?[4]

Such questions led King to weep over the laxity of the church. Yet his tears were tears of concern, for he loved the sacred walls of the church, and he saw her as the body of Christ. The church was, for him, the beloved community. Unfortunately, because of failure to answer these searing questions, white Christians had "blemished and scarred that body through social neglect and fear of being nonconformist." As a result, the church had become a social club without social effectiveness. Sheltered under the anesthetizing security of stained-glass windows, she had become a taillight rather than a headlight leading the world to higher levels of justice. Her leaders had retreated into pious irrelevancies and sanctimonious trivialities.

This indictment applied not just to conservative Christians but also to self-styled moderates and liberals. While they professed to be on the side of justice, they were shallow in their thinking, leaving King more frustrated than with those people of ill will who had absolutely misunderstood what was at stake. Lukewarm acceptance was "much more bewildering than outright rejection."[5] Moreover, the readiness of moderates to accuse him of extremism simply showed that they had failed to come to terms with the challenge of Jesus' command to love. Consequently the church stood under the judgment of God.

This had not always been the story of the church. King puts the issue nicely:

4. Washington, ed., *Testament of Hope*, pp. 299-300.
5. Washington, ed., *Testament of Hope*, p. 295.

There was a time when the church was very powerful. It was during that period when the early Christians rejoiced when they were deemed worthy to suffer for what they believed. In those days the church was not merely a thermometer that recorded the ideas and principles of popular opinion; it was a thermostat that transformed the mores of society. When the early Christians entered a town the power structure got disturbed and immediately sought to convict them for being "disturbers of the peace" and "outside agitators." But they went on with the conviction that they were a "colony from heaven" and had to obey God rather than man. They were small in number but big in commitment. They were too God-intoxicated to be "astronomically intimidated." They brought an end to such ancient evils as infanticide and gladiatorial contest.[6]

Something of this bold, aggressive spirit had emerged with the African American church. Without abrogating their responsibility for their own lives and abandoning themselves to the passivity of victimhood, many of her leaders had stood up for justice. Now God was making his appeal through those committed to the cause of justice and freedom. As a result the African American church had become

a glorious example in the history of Christendom. For never in Christian history, within a Christian country, have Christian churches been on the receiving end of such naked brutality and violence as we are witnessing in America today. Not since the days of the catacombs has God's house, as a symbol, weathered such attacks as the Negro churches.[7]

King himself was very clear about his own dependence on the church. He was a minister of the gospel in the church; he had been nurtured in her bosom; he had been sustained by her spiritual blessings; and he would remain true to her "so long as the chord of life shall lengthen."[8]

6. Washington, ed., *Testament of Hope*, p. 300; cf. pp. 345-46.
7. Washington, ed., *Testament of Hope*, p. 347.
8. Washington, ed., *Testament of Hope*, p. 298.

While the secular press might ignore this dimension of his thought, for King the church was crucial in the struggle for justice.[9] Her faith, her liturgy, and the power at work in her midst were pivotal in his quest for social reform.[10] While King was happy to let the world eavesdrop on his message, that message was fundamentally theological in orientation and content. King's prescription at its core was that the church needed to enact her own fundamental convictions. This began with a proper grasp of the gospel:

> The gospel at its best deals with the whole man, not only his soul but his body, not only his spiritual well-being, but his material well-being. Any religion that professes to be concerned about the souls of men and is not concerned about the slums that damn them, the economic conditions that strangle them and the social conditions that cripple them is a spiritually moribund religion awaiting burial.[11]

Central, in turn, to the gospel is a God committed to justice:

> Those of us who call the name of Jesus Christ find something at the center of our faith which forever reminds us that God is on the side of

9. Richard John Neuhaus aptly captures this: "I recall rallies when, in the course of his preaching, King would hold forth on the theological and moral foundations of the movement. The klieg lights and cameras shut down, only to be turned on again when he returned to specifically political or programmatic themes. 'Watch the light,' he commented. 'They are not interested in the most important parts.'" See Neuhaus, "Remembering Martin Luther King, Jr.," *First Things*, October 2002, p. 97.

10. It is very important to remember that King's work was immersed in the liturgical rhythms of the African American church. He described one liturgical experience as "a glad echo of heaven itself." See Washington, ed., *Testament of Hope*, p. 435. His ability to evoke the significance of baptism is magnificently displayed in his account of the confrontation with Bull Connor, the racist police leader who set out to best him. "Bull Connor next would say, 'Turn the fire hoses on.' And as I said to you the other night, Bull Connor didn't know history. He knew a kind of physics that somehow didn't relate to the transphysics that we knew about. And that was the fact that there was a certain kind of fire that no water could put out. And we went before the fire hoses; we had known water. If we were Baptist or some other denomination, we had been immersed. If we were Methodist, and some others, we had been sprinkled, but we knew water." Washington, ed., *Testament of Hope*, p. 281.

11. Washington, ed., *Testament of Hope*, pp. 37-38.

truth and justice. Good Friday may occupy the throne for a day, but ultimately it must give way to the triumph of Easter. Evil may so shape events that Caesar will occupy a palace and Christ a cross, but that same Christ rose and split history into A.D. and B.C., so that even the life of Caesar must be dated by his name. Yes, the arc of the moral universe is long but it bends towards justice. There is something in this universe which justifies William Cullen Bryant in saying, "Truth crushed to earth will rise again." So in Montgomery, Alabama, we can walk and never grow weary, because we know that there will be a great camp meeting in the promised land of freedom and justice.[12]

On various occasions King spelled out the development of renewal as a series of steps in a costly process. Before identifying these steps, we must note that the classical Christian narrative of creation, fall, and redemption operated as the indispensable backdrop for these steps. Thus King appealed again and again to God's work in creating all persons in the image of God. He took with the utmost seriousness the inner, attitudinal, and spiritual woundedness of human beings. He returned ever and anew to the place of Jesus in the transformation of the world. He had a very strong sense of divine providence at work in history.[13] He readily looked forward in hope both to the personal survival of the individual after death and to the consummation of all things in the New Jerusalem.[14] Moreover, his own personal dependence on God was readily manifest at crucial points in his journey. The whole of King's positive prescription for change was, in fact, suffused with the themes of Scripture as read through the lens of creation and redemption. This was no mere rhetorical tactic or psychological device; it was integral to his very being. Hence

---

12. Washington, ed., *Testament of Hope*, p. 88; cf. pp. 141, 461.

13. In a wonderful turn of phrase, King once noted: ". . . I know, somehow, that only when it is dark enough, can you see the stars" (Washington, ed., *Testament of Hope*, p. 280); cf. "Whatever the name, some extra-human force labors to create a harmony out of the discord of the universe" (p. 438).

14. In his funeral eulogy for the little children who were killed on 15 September 1963, King averred, "Death is not a period that ends the great sentence of life, but a comma that punctuates it to more lofty significance." Washington, ed., *Testament of Hope*, p. 222.

his proposals for change were rooted in the gospel and in the version of liberal Protestantism that he had worked out for himself.

In the march towards justice and freedom, as that applied to the problem of race, King saw the church as needing to accomplish four things. First, she must expose the ideational and spiritual roots of the problem. Drawing where possible on scholarly inquiry, the religious education of the church should give direction to the popular mind. Second, the church should use her resources to reveal the true intentions of African Americans by challenging irrational fears and telling the truth about the campaign for civil rights. Third, the church needs to keep people centered on God. In particular she should make clear the eternal demands of God and constantly remind the church that she is a colony of heaven. Fourth, the church must lead in social reform, moving out from the realm of ideas into social action. Clearly, the church needed to remove the yoke of segregation from its own body:

> Unfortunately most of the major denominations still practice segregation in local churches, hospitals, schools, and other church institutions. It is appalling that the most segregated hour of Christian America is eleven o'clock on Sunday morning, the same hour when many are standing to sing, "In Christ there is no East and West." Equally appalling is the fact that the most segregated school of the week is the Sunday School. How often the church has had a high blood count on creeds and an anemia on deeds![15]

Extending this reform to the social and political arena, the church needed to fuse the ethic of Jesus with the tactic of nonviolent action. Here the inspiration, of course, was Mahatma Gandhi, but King was very clear on his priorities: "Nonviolence had emerged as the technique of the movement, while love stood as the regulating ideal. In other words, Christ furnished the spirit and motivation, while Gandhi furnished the method."[16] In a similar way, King skillfully and relentlessly appealed to

---

15. Washington, ed., *Testament of Hope*, p. 479.
16. Washington, ed., *Testament of Hope*, p. 447.

the American dream of democracy. His famous "I have a Dream" address at the Lincoln Memorial on 28 August 1963 brilliantly suffused the narratives of faith and nation, switching back and forth from the language of Scripture to the language of national mythology as if they were a seamless whole.[17]

By the end of his life, King had stretched his litany of problems beyond that of race to that of national poverty, to the Vietnam War, back to the Arab-Israeli conflict, and then out to the plight of the despised and poor everywhere.[18] Yet he never wavered in his primary theological and spiritual horizons. He insisted that human laws were subordinate to divine law. In explaining his own ministry, he broke loose from the purely empirical and humanistic categories that were intellectually so attractive to him.[19] Even when trying to forge the idea of a unifying principle of life that could be owned by Hindus, Muslims, Jews, Christians, and Buddhists, his center of gravity remained rooted in the first epistle of John: "Let us love one another; for love is of God and everyone that loves is born of God and knows God."[20] At the end he was preaching with characteristic flair in a leading Pentecostal church the same faith that had sustained him across his turbulent ministry.

In King we have one of the most important visions of renewal to surface in the twentieth century. The fundamental problem turns out, in this instance, to be moral: modern American society and the modern white American church are riddled with injustice. The solution is spiritual and theological. The church must recover her nerve and implement the gospel by adopting a costly discipline of nonviolent action that will appeal to the conscience of racists, warmongers, oppressors, and the like. There can be no retreat into "some inner spiritual church, the church within the church, as the true ecclesia and the hope of the world."[21] We must live

---

17. His wife once commented, "At that moment it seemed as if the Kingdom of God appeared. But it lasted only for a moment." Washington, ed., *Testament of Hope*, p. 217.

18. King proposed very specific solutions to all these problems.

19. "So every rational explanation breaks down at some point. There is something about the protest [in Montgomery] that is suprarational; it cannot be explained without a divine dimension." See Washington, ed., *Testament of Hope*, p. 438.

20. 1 John 4:7.

21. Washington, ed., *Testament of Hope*, p. 300.

and work in the church as she is in history. As we do so, the power of God will make present the kingdom of God in the midst of history. As co-workers with God, we can still hope that the Christian era at long last will be established in the world. In the meantime, we must come down from the mountaintop, where we have seen the coming of the Lord, and suffer in the struggle for justice across the face of the earth.

King died in the service of this vision. So too did Archbishop Oscar Romero, the other renewalist I want to explore in this chapter. They had other characteristics in common: both were pastors, both were beloved leaders in their communities, both received international honors, both were deeply concerned about the poor, and both have been hailed as martyrs. Romero's vision of renewal is similar in many ways to King's, yet the differences in background, content, style, and strategy are instructive.

Before becoming archbishop, Romero was a conservative figure in the Roman Catholic Church in El Salvador. Like King, he stumbled into renewal, thrown into profound personal change by the injustice, corrupt politics, and terrorism that engulfed his country in the 1970s. The initial cause of his transformation from genial conservative to reforming renewalist was the brutality experienced by his priests and people at the hands of the government, the military, and the capitalistic barons who controlled the economy. The problem was at once civil and ecclesial: conservative politicians and church leaders stood idly by, or gladly collaborated with, acts of brutal injustice. Romero's solution was to embrace and implement the vision of renewal adopted at Vatican II as developed to fit local circumstances by the Latin American bishops at their regional conferences at Medellin and Puebla.

He shared that solution in a series of four well-crafted pastoral letters to his archdiocese. As one works through the letters in order, one can see that Romero gradually developed his vision of change as he responded to the various crises in El Salvador. As we will note later, a fascinating ambivalence emerges over time in the role he assigns to the poor. Otherwise, there is a gradual evolution and well-rounded consistency in his position.

The First Pastoral Letter grounded his work firmly in the faith of the Catholic church, as that faith was reaffirmed at Vatican II and articulated by Pope Paul VI. The pattern is simple. In and through Easter, God has visited and redeemed the world in Christ. The risen Lord continues his redemptive work in human history in and through his body, the church: ". . . the whole purpose of the church's existence is to make obvious and operative, in the midst of humanity, the abundant energy of the death and resurrection of the Lord."[22] The church in turn serves the world, making the world the beneficiary of Easter. In doing so, the church must be clear about the primacy of its own spiritual mission. Yet the church enters into conversation and dialogue with the world, for she has a high conception of human persons, and she is committed to the liberation of the suffering neighbor. This is clearly a conventional, top-down conception of ministry. Yet two things are immediately apparent. First, Romero was not simply a traditionalist cleric; he had imbibed the new spirit of Vatican II in which the institutions of the church were to be suffused with a personalist and social vision of the gospel. Second, he was deadly serious about entering into dialogue both with clergy and laity in the church and with politicians and others concerned about the welfare of the people of El Salvador. Progressives were delighted about the second of these developments; rigid and fearful conservatives were alarmed.

In Romero's Second Pastoral Letter, we begin to feel the pulse of the archbishop. We can also see him edging his way aggressively towards the full-blown vision that emerges in the fourth. Thus, he concentrates on the church's mission in the world, pressing hard for the need to come to terms with contemporary social and political reality:

> . . . the tradition that Christ entrusted to his church is not a museum of souvenirs to be protected. It is true that the tradition comes out of the past, and that it ought to be loved and faithfully preserved. But it has always a view to the future. It is a tradition that makes the church new, up to date, effective in every historical epoch. It is a tradition that nourishes the church's hope and faith so that it may go on preaching, so that it may invite all men and women to the "new heaven and new earth" that God has promised (Rev. 21:1; Isa. 65:17).[23]

22. Archbishop Oscar Romero, *The Voice of the Voiceless* (New York: Orbis, 1985), p. 57.
23. Romero, *Voice of the Voiceless*, p. 69.

Interestingly, Romero here switches the order of presentation, so that the mission of the church to the world comes before the material on the nature of the church. And in the later sections he skillfully picks up the proclamation and manifestation of the kingdom of God as the heart of Christ's preaching and teaching. Within this, he highlights Christ's preference for the poor as a constitutive element of the church's vocation to continue the work of Jesus.

> This preference of Jesus for the poor stands out throughout the gospel. It was for them that he worked his cures and exorcisms; he lived and ate with them; he united himself with, defended, and encouraged all those who, in his day, were on the margin of society, whether for social or for religious reasons: sinners, publicans, prostitutes, Samaritans, lepers. This closeness of Jesus to those who were marginalized is the sign that he gives to confirm the content of what he preaches: the kingdom of God is at hand.[24]

Romero was well aware of the objections his proposals had already roused. Thus the archdiocese had been accused of preaching hatred and subversion, of being Marxist, and of overstepping the limits of the church's mission by meddling in politics. He dealt with these objections head on, noting the brutal persecution the church was facing. The note of realism is striking: "The most serious persecution of the church is that which makes it impossible for it to carry out its mission, and which attacks those to whom its word of salvation is directed."[25] He looked upon persecution as inevitable, given the church's commitment to the kingdom of God and to truth. Moreover, he fully recognized the danger to the unity of the church from those who were anchored in a false traditionalism.

> When the church enters into the world of sin to liberate and save it, the sin of the world enters into the church and divides it: it separates

24. Romero, *Voice of the Voiceless*, p. 71.
25. Romero, *Voice of the Voiceless*, p. 79.

those who are authentically Christian and persons of good will from those who are Christian only in name and appearance.[26]

The Third Pastoral Letter was even more specific in its treatment of issues pertinent to the mission of the church in El Salvador. Working with Bishop Arturo y Damas, bishop of Santiago de Maria, Romero explored in fine detail the relation between the church and popular organizations. They also carefully articulated the church's teaching on violence. As to the former, he provided a careful account of the social, political, and spiritual situation that evoked the emergence of popular organizations. Within the church, he welcomed the arrival of basic ecclesial communities of Bible study, prayer, and contextual reflection on action and ministry: "These communities have to be maintained and strengthened because they are the vital cells of the church. They embody the whole concept of the church and its unique mission."[27] Outside the church, he insisted that people had the right to form trade unions, political parties, and organizations, even thought it was vital that the faith of the gospel not be collapsed or reduced to political action. He analyzed the various forms of violence at work in society, and he defended the church's general teaching that permitted violence in cases of self-defense and insurrection. The letter ends with a call to the public authorities to obey the voice of Christ as set out in a series of six very specific demands and with an assurance that the church would remain faithful to its identity.[28]

It is in the Fourth Pastoral Letter that the full contours of Romero's vision of renewal emerge. By this time, Romero had committed himself to the language of crisis. By this time also, all the bishops of Latin America had met in council at Puebla. Romero knitted the fresh message developed there with his earlier pastoral letters, with the material from the

26. Romero, *Voice of the Voiceless*, p. 81.

27. Romero, *Voice of the Voiceless*, p. 96.

28. The demands at issue were: 1. Pass laws that take account of the majority of Salvadorans in the countryside. 2. Widen the arena of political discussion. 3. Provide legal opportunity to organize for those excluded from discussion, especially the poor. 4. Repeal the Law for the Defense and Guarantee of the Public Order. 5. Stop terrorization of the rural poor. 6. Win the confidence of the people by appropriate means. Romero, *Voice of the Voiceless*, pp. 111-12.

bishops' earlier council at Medellin, and with the documents developed at Vatican II and thereafter.[29] The letter operated both as an end in itself and as an introduction to the report of the Puebla conference of bishops.

The root issue facing the nation of El Salvador was that of injustice. Romero catalogued the manifestations of this injustice both in general terms and in graphic detail. He charted a litany of evils in society generally, in the political arena, in government attitude and policy, in the economic sphere, and in public and private life. Within the church he charted a crisis that was manifest in internal disunity and polarization, in a failure of renewal and adaptation, and in a disregard for the criteria of political involvement laid down in the gospel. Overall, we might say that the diagnosis of his situation was moral, spiritual, and theological. The church, faced with the challenge of widespread injustice and evil, had come to reflect the polarization of the society as a whole, had not kept up with the best wisdom and guidance of the modern church, and had, in its own efforts for renewal, politically and ideologically adulterated the gospel. The solution clearly had to be morally, spiritually, and theologically comprehensive. The core of the solution was for the church to continue its commitment to the liberation of the people of El Salvador.

We can summarize Romero's prescription in a bundle of imperatives that are laid out in part two of the letter. I provide my own list as a way of capturing Romero's convictions: 1. The church must be true to its own identity and transcendent mission. 2. The church should commit itself to integral evangelization, that is, to a complex, liberating transformation of the whole of life.[30] 3. In its evangelization, the church must sustain its doctrinal moorings, sticking to the truth about Christ, the church, and humankind, and attending to the church's social teachings. 4. The church has the mission of "denouncing every lie, every injustice, every sin that

29. The deliberations of a worldwide Bishops' Conference in Rome that resulted in *Evangelii Nuntiandi* and that was promulgated by Pope Paul VI on 5 December 1975 was clearly critical to Romero's work as a whole. It is a landmark document in the history of evangelism and mission. It is available in several places on the Internet.

30. Note that "evangelization" in Roman Catholic circles is not confined, say, to proclamation, catechesis, or personal conversion, as is often the case in Protestant circles. The full vision is spelled out in *Evangelii Nuntiandi*.

destroys God's plan."[31] In prophetic witness, the church should unmask the idolatries manifest in the absolutization of wealth and private property, of national security, and of political and popular organizations. 5. The church must promote integral human liberation, "being 'the voice of the voiceless,' a defender of the rights of the poor, a promoter of every just aspiration for liberation, a guide, an empowerer, a humanizer of every legitimate struggle to achieve a more just society, a society that prepares the way for the true kingdom of God in history."[32] 6. The church should preach and encourage the urgent need for profound structural changes in the social and political arena. 7. The church should share in the life of the people, both masses and elites, acting as salt, light, and leaven.

In part three of the letter, Romero revisits the problem of violence, the engagement with Marxism,[33] and the complexities of national dialogue. Part four closes out the letter by dealing with the pastoral application of the Puebla report to the archdiocese of El Salvador. Here he reiterates the evolving nature of the church, the preferential option for the poor, and the importance of unity in spirit and action. He presses home again the need to evangelize the masses, the importance of basic ecclesial communities, and the commitment to accompany those Christians called to serve in the political arena.

Romero offered the core elements of this vision of renewal in his visit to the governing board of the National Council of Churches in November 1979, where his vision got the attention of many mainline Christian leaders in the United States. He also reiterated it at an important lecture in Louvain in February 1980. What is striking about this lecture is that the

---

31. Romero, *Voice of the Voiceless*, p. 132.

32. Romero, *Voice of the Voiceless*, p. 138.

33. He deftly used the evasive passive to show his critical engagement with the Marxist tradition. Noting that the church rejects Marxism as an atheistic ideology, he continued, "It can be understood as a scientific analysis of the economic and social order. Many in El Salvador, as elsewhere in Latin America, use this analysis as a scientific tool because, they claim, it in no way affects their religious principles. The magisterium of the church (in *Octogenesis Adveniens*, for example), although it recognizes the distinction between Marxism as an ideology and as a scientific method, prudently warns of possible ideological risks." Romero, *Voice of the Voiceless*, p. 146.

idea of a preferential option for the poor has clearly come to occupy a much more pronounced place than had heretofore been the case in Romero's public declarations. In particular, he insists that the poor provide a privileged position intellectually for understanding the gospel. We can read this change in one of two ways. On the one hand, we can see it as representing the true mind of Romero, with his pastoral letters reflecting his mind as constrained by the official teaching of the magisterium. Alternatively, we can read it as a natural evolution from his earlier deliberations. We need not decide this here, but it is important to lay out the shift in content with some care.[34]

In his pastoral letters it is clear that the preferential option for the poor plays a decisive role in Romero's vision of renewal. He comes back to it again and again. Overall, the option for the poor is seen partly in theological terms and partly in moral terms. Given that it is constitutive in the ministry of Jesus, it continues to be constitutive for his continued ministry in the church today; thus it is an element in Romero's Christology and ecclesiology. Yet it is also constitutive of the Christian's love of the neighbor. Romero is very careful, however, to balance this commitment with two qualifications: the ministry of the church is not exclusively to the poor, and there is nothing ontologically or epistemologically privileged about the poor. Consider the following cautions:

> . . . the church, like Jesus, has to go on proclaiming the good news that the kingdom is at hand, especially for the great majority who, in worldly terms, have been estranged from it — the poor, the low-income classes, the marginalized. This does not mean that the church should neglect the other classes in society. It wants to serve them also, to enlighten them. It also needs their help in building up the kingdom. But the church should share Jesus' preference for those who have been used for others' interest and have not been in control of their own destinies.[35]

34. In his very helpful essay on Romero, Jon Sobrino takes the latter view. See his "A Theologian's View of Oscar Romero," Romero, *Voice of the Voiceless*, pp. 22-51.

35. Romero, *Voice of the Voiceless*, p. 74.

The church does not approve of the poor and the oppressed simply because they are poor and oppressed — though it cannot forget that the Redeemer himself offered the grace of redemption to them first of all. The church knows perfectly well that among those that lack material goods there is a great deal of sinfulness. It therefore makes every effort to see that persons are saved from their inveterate vices, many of which are fomented by our historical situation. In the name of the preferential option for the poor there can never be justification of the machismo, the alcoholism, the failure of family responsibility, the exploitation of one poor person by another, the antagonism among neighbors, and the many other sins that our survey pointed to strongly as being current roots of this country's crisis and violence.[36]

Note here how the subject or agent of the action and knowing is invariably the church. Now consider in this catena of quotations how the poor have become the agents of the action and knowing:

. . . we say of the world of the poor that it is the key to understanding the Christian faith, to understanding the activity of the church and the political dimension of that faith and that ecclesial action. It is the poor who tell us what the world is, and what the church's service to the world should be. It is the poor who tell us what the *polis* is, what the city is and what it means for the church really to live in the world.[37]

Our encounter with the poor has regained for us the central truth of the gospel, through which the word of God urges us to conversion.[38]

Here again we find the same key to understanding the persecution of the church: the poor. Once again it is the poor who bring us to understand what has really happened. That is why the church has understood the persecution from the perspective of the poor.[39]

36. Romero, *Voice of the Voiceless*, p. 140.
37. Romero, *Voice of the Voiceless*, p. 179.
38. Romero, *Voice of the Voiceless*, p. 180.
39. Romero, *Voice of the Voiceless*, p. 182.

The transcendence of the gospel has guided us in our judgment and in our action. But it is also true that, to look at it another way, that the faith itself has been deepened, that hidden riches of the gospel have been opened, precisely by taking up this stance toward socio-political reality such as it is.[40]

I have tried to make clear to you the ultimate criterion, one which is theological and historical, for the church's involvement in the world of the poor. In accordance with its own specific nature the church will go on supporting one or another political program to the extent that it operates in favor of the poor among the people.[41]

Early Christians used to say *Gloria Dei, vivens homo* ("the glory of God is the living person"). We could make this more concrete by say-ing *Gloria Dei, vivens pauper* ("the glory of God is the living poor person"). From the perspective of the transcendence of the gospel, I believe we can determine what the life of the poor truly is. And I also believe that by putting ourselves alongside the poor and trying to bring new life to them we shall come to know the eternal truth of the gospel.[42]

If we take these quotations seriously, then we have an amended vision of renewal. The presenting problem remains that of injustice in the world. Moreover, encountering this injustice exposed the church's dis-unity, her refusal to be abreast of the best wisdom of her Councils, and of the ideological adulteration of the gospel. The initial solution was to con-tinue a commitment to the liberation of the people of El Salvador; clearly this was a very particular solution focused on one country. But then the solution was transposed and universalized. In seeking to liberate the poor and oppressed in El Salvador, the church had discovered in the poor an

40. Romero, *Voice of the Voiceless*, p. 183. Romero goes on to spell out the material con-tent of these hidden riches in terms of a clearer awareness of sin, greater clarity on the In-carnation and redemption, and a deeper faith in God and in Christ.

41. Romero, *Voice of the Voiceless*, p. 186.

42. Romero, *Voice of the Voiceless*, p. 187.

epistemic site for understanding the eternal truth of the gospel. Note here that the poor are not an originating source of the gospel; the cognitive help given is interpretive or hermeneutical in nature. Nor is it the case that the poor themselves furnish the help given; it is the church that comes to know the hidden treasures of the gospel. Nevertheless, this is a very substantial claim that needs to be pondered with great care.

What can we glean from these similar yet contrasting proposals?

First, if we focus initially on the problem of race and the effort to respond to it resolutely, then it is clear that the renewalist vision of Martin Luther King Jr. has been spectacularly successful. This is not to claim that racism has been overcome, or that there are no racists in the modern church. It is to say that the issue of racial bigotry and discrimination is resolved and closed. While this resolution may have been the fruit of King's wobbly liberal Protestantism, it also clearly springs deep from within the gospel preached from the beginning within the African American community, and it also emerges naturally from the classical and canonical faith of the church. Thus it belongs now to the whole church.

We cannot be as enthusiastic, however, for the particular method King used to achieve renewal, namely pacifism coupled with aggressive protest and legislative action. Here the events of the last generation show Romero to be a wiser counselor. His position on violence is much more persuasive in the light of forms of terrorism and violence that cannot find purchase in the conscience of their agents. King, like Gandhi, was able to succeed because his opponents had to acknowledge subjectively the justice of his cause.

Second, we can also say that the wider commitment to justice is nonnegotiable. In this regard, it is clear that the arrival of God's kingdom is central to the recovery of the gospel today. The hard, even offensive, language is important. We need the language of the kingdom precisely because it draws attention to the social, political, and historical dimensions of the Christian faith. The cross and resurrection of Jesus is a turning point in history in part because it was a standing challenge to the injustice of Caesar and the powers that be. Any vision of renewal that sidelines these aspects of the faith will be weak and anemic.

Third, matters are more complicated in the call for a preferential option for the poor. On the one hand, a church that does not minister to the poor is simply failing to follow and imitate her Lord and Savior. This is utterly sufficient warrant to supply the marching orders for ministry in this arena. On the other hand, it is fascinating how once again a proposal for renewal winds up in a seminar in the philosophy department. We have been led once more into the murky waters of epistemology. Outside the impressive personal testimony of experience and martyrdom, Romero provides no good reason for this transposition in his vision. As we saw in the case of Ratzinger, the epistemology on offer is a version of a more general epistemology canonized by the Roman Catholic Church. We may justly wonder if the cognitive promises attached to this dimension of the proposal will survive scrutiny.

Fourth, we cannot fail to note the crucial place that base communities and parachurch organizations have in the renewal of the church. For both King and Romero they had a pivotal place in the economy and practice of renewal. Whatever the difficulties such groups bring with them, they are indispensable in the comprehensive renewal of the church. They provide a place for much needed conversation and reflection, they make discoveries unlikely to be made within conventional establishments, and they can experiment with the retrieval and invention of practices that bring healthy change.

This has been a happy chapter overall; it has ended on a note of resounding success in renewal. Yet we need to add a couple of important observations in closing. In working for the renewal of the church, one can be killed. One can also develop a false sense of assurance. After all, having gotten one big issue right, it is tempting to think that one will then get everything else right. Our propensity for self-deception is an enduring one. It is now all too customary for adherents of this or that cause to find a way to cast virtually every issue in the church as one of justice, inclusion, victimhood, and race. The hope is that the success of the past will cast a halo merely by being associated with the new cause. This is a shallow practice, one that tarnishes those who deploy it and inhibits rather than furthers the cause of renewal. Hence we need to press on and find a fresh theme that will so absorb us that we shall be drawn away from this temptation. We can find it by turning to the topic of liturgical renewal and by examining two voices that are less celebrated than King and Romero. We shall also continue our respite from the worries about issues of truth and justification.

CHAPTER 6

TROJAN HORSES FROM PARIS

ALEXANDER SCHMEMANN AND GILBERT BILEZIKIAN

MOST RENEWALISTS HAVE BECOME household names in the contemporary church, but two who have yet to achieve this distinction are Alexander Schmemann (1921-1983) and Gilbert Bilezikian (1930-). For the most part they represent voices behind the scenes. As their foreign-sounding names might suggest, Schmemann and Bilezikian were not born in the United States, even though their impact there has been profound. Born in Estonia and brought up in Paris, Schmemann lived and worked in New York; Bilezikian's parents originated in Armenia, but he was born and raised in Paris, and he lived and worked in Chicago. In both instances their reflections on renewal began with the liturgical life of the church. In time, they moved beyond this arena to develop full-fledged visions of a renewed church that focused on the sense of the church as a distinct self-identifying community. Yet they present radically different historical visions of the church across her history. As we work our way through their positions, we shall see that they present some very stark choices in any comprehensive and critical vision of renewal. We begin with Schmemann.

There has been a long-standing reluctance to write about renewal within the Eastern Orthodox tradition. There are at least three reasons for the reticence. First, renewal has been systematically institutionalized twice over within the tradition. Thus renewal is embodied in the monasteries that have had a profound influence in the tradition as a whole. Further, the whole experience of Lent within Eastern Orthodoxy is surely geared to fostering personal, spiritual renewal. Second, Eastern Orthodox church leaders are acutely aware of the pathology of renewal. They instinctively sense the dangers of excess, especially as they observe how various renewal efforts in the West have led to the erosion of precious treasures of the faith, have fostered judgmentalism against others, and have led to terrible division in the body faithful. Third, there is a pervasive spiritual ethos within Eastern Orthodoxy that inhibits its leaders from going public on issues of renewal. In this understanding of things, we should leave renewal to God. The problems the church faces are really too complex to be solved by human ingenuity, and it is much better to attend to our own sins than to be preoccupied with the sins of the wider church.

Against this backdrop, Schmemann's substantial contribution to renewal is all the more interesting and important. Originally published in Russian, the central material appeared in English in his book, *The Eucharist: Sacrament of the Kingdom*, sometime after his death. Schmemann went so far, in fact, as to speak of a crisis in the church:

> . . . this crisis consists of a lack of connection and cohesion between what is accomplished in the eucharist and how it is perceived, understood and lived. To a certain degree this crisis has always existed in the Church. The life of the Church, or rather the people of the Church, has never been perfect, ideal. With time, however, this crisis has become chronic. That schizophrenia that poisons the life of the Church and undermines its very foundations has come to be seen as a normal state.[1]

The crisis Schmemann was fundamentally concerned to address is liturgical; it had to do with the central act of worship in the church, the Eucharist. To be sure, he also believed that there is a crisis in the wider culture in the West. There is hatred, division, bloodshed, and rebellion against God; ideology and utopian escapism are rampant. These have in-

---

1. Alexander Schmemann, *The Eucharist: Sacrament of the Kingdom* (Crestwood, New York: St. Vladimir's Seminary Press, 1988), p. 9.

fected Western Christianity to the point where theologies of liberation ensure that economics, politics, and psychology have displaced the common Christian vision of God. However, attending to the cultural crisis is penultimate. First and foremost, attention needs to be given to the inner life of the church, especially to her eucharistic life. This might make it appear that for Schmemann the issue was narrowly focused on just one aspect of the church's life. In fact, eucharistic practice was the doorway into a whole network of problems facing the church. We can usefully explore his position by separating primary and secondary issues.

The primary problem is a loss of ecclesial consciousness as Christians gather at the Eucharist. Originally, Christians entered into a profound encounter with God in the Sunday assembly. There was a real sense of mutual interdependence. Together they made an ascent to the table of the Lord in his kingdom and there encountered the Holy Spirit and the fullness of grace. The problem in the contemporary church is that this sense of corporate unity around the Eucharist has disappeared from the life of the church. In turn this liturgical malpractice, this loss of corporate togetherness, has led to a series of debilitating secondary developments. There are six of these in all for Schmemann.

First, theology has been cut off from the lived experience of the church and works independently with its own *a priori* categories. Not surprisingly, we encounter school theology, or scholasticism. Second, liturgical piety has become entirely individualistic. Rather than being a corporate ascent into the kingdom of God, communion is now seen as a place to find consolation, comfort, and help. Third, the eucharistic liturgy has been divided up into various parts; then some parts, like the words of institution, have been demarcated as sacred, receiving intense interest and attention. The result is liturgical reductionism. Fourth, a false symbolism that treats what is happening in the liturgy as symbolic rather than real is generated. Thus the liturgy becomes a kind of make-believe world of its own. Fifth, a false split between clergy and laity has developed. Essentially the clergy are there to provide services for the laity. The clergy serve; the laity pray. The clergy are the initiated; the laity are the uninitiated. The clergy are first class citizens; the laity are second class citizens. This loss of togetherness has spilled over into church architecture: the iconostasis has become a wall of separation between clergy and laity. Sixth, and finally, the church has become cut off from the world. Rather than being a place where created elements are brought and transformed by the Holy Spirit, the church has becomes a place of escape from the world. Salvation has become escapism rather than the transformation of the whole of created existence.

If the problem begins with a loss of ecclesial consciousness around the Eucharist, then clearly the solution must be in this arena as well:

> I am convinced that the genuine revival of the Church begins with *eucharistic revival*, but in the fullness of the word. The tragic flaw in the history of Orthodoxy has been proven to be not only the incompleteness but, I daresay, the absence of a theology of the sacraments, its reduction into western schemes and categories of thought. The Church is not an organization but the new people of God. The Church is not a religious cult but a *liturgy*, embracing the entire creation of God. The Church is not a doctrine about the world to come but the joyous encounter of the kingdom of God. It is the sacrament of peace, the sacrament of salvation, and the sacrament of the reign of Christ.[2]

Rather than turn our attention to the various problems of culture, we need to turn

> . . . to the sacrament of the eucharist and to the church, whose very life flows from the sacrament. Yes, I do believe that precisely here, in this holy of holies of the Church, in this ascent to the table of the Lord in his kingdom, is the source of the renewal of which we hope. And I do believe, as the Church has always believed, that this upward journey begins with "the laying aside of all earthly cares," with leaving this adulterous and sinful world. No ideological fuss and bother, but a gift from heaven — such is the vocation of the Church in the world, the source of his service.

2. Schmemann, *Eucharist,* p. 242 (emphasis in the original).

I also believe that, by God's grace, Orthodoxy throughout all the ages has kept and guarded this vision, this consciousness of the Church, this knowledge that "where the Church is, there is the Holy Spirit and fullness of grace" (Irenaeus of Lyons, Against the Heresies 3:24:1). But precisely because this is so, we the Orthodox faithful must find the inner strength to plunge into the Eucharistic renewal of the Church. It is not reform, adjustments, and modernization that are needed so much as a return to that vision and experience that from the beginning constituted the very life of the Church.[3]

We can see here a natural match between the problem and the solution. Thus if the core of the problem is related to eucharistic vision and practice, the solution must also take place in and around the Eucharist. This is not a narrowing of the problem, because for Schmemann, "everything pertaining to the Eucharist pertains to the Church, and everything pertaining to the Church pertains to the Eucharist and is *tested* by its interdependence."[4] Moreover, the Eucharist is not mere symbolic action. In and through the whole liturgy there is a manifestation of the Holy Spirit. In and through the whole Eucharist there is an ascent to the kingdom of God, into the holy of holies. In and through the Eucharist, we are in touch with the manifestation of the victory of the kingdom of God, and we participate in eternal life. In fact, we gain *true* knowledge of God, not simply *rational* knowledge of God.

Once we work through this primary problem of ecclesial conscious-

3. Schmemann, *Eucharist*, p. 10.

4. Schmemann, *Eucharist*, p. 215 (emphasis in the original). Elsewhere Schmemann makes this point as follows: "Christian faith begins with the encounter with Christ, with the reception of him as the Son of God, who manifests the Father and his love to us. This acceptance of the Son, this union in him with the Father, is fulfilled as salvation, as the new life, as the kingdom of God in the communion of the Holy Spirit, which is the divine life itself, divine love itself, communion with God. And thus, the eucharist is also the sacrament of our *access* to God and knowledge of him and union with him. Being offered in the Son, it is offered to the Father. Being offered to the Father, it is fulfilled in the participation of the Holy Spirit. And therefore the eucharist is the eternally living and life-creating source of the Church's knowledge of the Most Holy Trinity. This is not the abstract knowledge (of dogmas, doctrine) that it unfortunately remains for so many of the faithful, but knowledge as a genuine *recognition*, as meeting, as experience, and thus as participating of life eternal." Schmemann, *Eucharist*, pp. 167-68 (emphasis in the original).

ness in and around the Eucharist, the other secondary problems will more or less take care of themselves. Thus, creation will be bathed in the kingdom. We will recover a sense of the unity between clergy and laity. We will abandon bad theories of symbol, as these relate to the liturgy. We will retrieve the unity of the liturgy itself, abandoning the practice of reducing it to particular bits and pieces according to some scheme of the sacred. We will also recover a sense of the unity of the whole assembly in worship. In time we will also begin to produce much better theology, including much better liturgical and biblical theology.

So the solution to the crisis in the contemporary church as Schmemann envisaged it was this: as Christians gather in assembly to celebrate the Eucharist together as one people, they should come to terms with the manifestation of the Holy Spirit in their midst drawing them into the kingdom of God. From this center emanates the intellectual resources and energy that will overcome the secondary network of problems that have emerged in the wake of the loss of ecclesial consciousness. Thus we can challenge the reigning scholasticism in theology and the invidious individualism in the celebration of the liturgy. We can begin again to see the liturgy as a whole and abandon bad theories of symbolism that treat the liturgy as a kind of make-believe world. We can overcome the split between clergy and laity and we can look for the renewal of the whole of creation. The energy for these changes is not self-produced; it is supplied by the presence of the Holy Spirit here and now in the church and in the world.

As we will see, on the surface this way of seeing things may seem very far removed from the vision of the second figure we shall look at it in this chapter. And it is hard to see the happy-clappy liturgies of contemporary Protestantism as in any way related to the canonical liturgies of the church championed by Schmemann. It is difficult to see any connection between the highly formal tradition of Eastern Orthodoxy and the radically innovative practices of contemporary Protestantism. Frankly, it strains credulity to look for analogies or continuities between Alexander Schmemann and Gilbert Bilezikian.

Yet we must move cautiously and not jump prematurely to conclusions. Schmemann once noted that in ecumenical gatherings, it was common for the conference organizers to place him beside either Roman Catholics or Anglo-Catholics. He himself would have been entirely happy to sit beside the Quakers, for he shared their deep dependence on the presence and work of the Holy Spirit.[5] Equally, it is important to keep our historical wits about us. Again and again Protestantism has reached back to the Eucharist as central in renewal. Consider the awakenings in Ulster in the 1620s that began with careful preparation for communion in the congregations of the Scotch-Irish. Think of the pivotal place of eucharistic practice in the camp-meeting tradition of early Methodism in North America. Ponder the place of the Eucharist in the Anglo-Catholic renewal of the nineteenth century. Bear in mind also the present importance of the Eucharist for the Cursillo and Walk to Emmaus Movements. There are deep correlations between Protestantism and Eastern Orthodoxy below the surface that link up with the proposals of Schmemann.

In fact, the work in renewal that is intimately related to the theological innovations of Gilbert Bilezikian began with a liturgical crisis. Here the presenting problem was the boredom and irrelevance of conventional worship for a youth group. The group had been led by Bill Hybels, Bilezikian's best known student and collaborator.[6] The innovations developed by Hybels were pretty dramatic. Thus when they met in the sanctuary, they staged creative competitions that went all the way "from Frisbee throws down the center aisle to 'challenge the champ' spectaculars, which could have provided ideas for the *Guinness Book of Records*."[7] In time, Hybels determined to develop a service designed for seekers that would be a safe place where "they could come week after week and hear the dangerous, life-transforming message of Christ."[8] Not surprisingly, this did not

5. I owe this observation to personal conversation with Archbishop Dimitri of Dallas and the South.

6. The details are well supplied in Lynne and Bill Hybels, *Rediscovering Church: The Story and Vision of Willow Creek Community Church* (Grand Rapids: Zondervan, 1995), pp. 28-32.

7. Hybels and Hybels, *Rediscovering Church*, p. 36.

8. Hybels and Hybels, *Rediscovering Church*, p. 40. A description of the service that led to the decision to make seekers central in the life of the church is instructive. "The night came and there were kids hanging out the windows. Nearly six hundred charged-up stu-

fit well with the conventions of the local congregation in which they were located. As it happened, this experiment in youth ministry coincided with Hybels's exposure to the teaching of Bilezikian who challenged him and other students to follow the model of church life laid out in Acts 2.[9]

Beginning on 12 October 1975 Hybels, Bilezikian, and others began a new congregation in the Willow Creek Theater in the suburbs of Chicago. By 1981, they had moved into a permanent facility. In between, the new community nearly fell apart because of a catalogue of problems: an insane pace of life, immature leadership, financial stress, clinical depression, and imbalanced teaching. Over time, however, the leaders stabilized their mission and practices. Their continued and continuing success in reaching outsiders with the gospel has meant that thousands have since beaten a path to their door. In turn, Hybels, Bilezikian, and other team leaders have taken their proposals about how to be the church across the globe. They have even been featured in a seminar setting in the Harvard Business School.[10]

Bilezikian supplies the theological resources for Willow Creek.[11]

---

dents filled the church auditorium, and everything — from the opening jam (our version of a prelude) to the prayer at the end — was designed just for them. We had great contemporary music, sidesplitting drama, a powerful media presentation, and moving lead-in music. Then Bill walked out in jeans and a T-shirt with an open Bible in his hands. 'Let me read you the greatest story in the history of the world,' he said. 'It's about a God-man named Jesus.' Then he read the story of the crucifixion and made some comments. At the end of the message, he said, 'The reason Jesus did what he did is that He knows that kids like you have rebelled and sinned against Him, even at your relatively young ages. But you still matter to God. So He sent His Son to die in your place. If you'd like to receive Him now, stand to your feet.' So many kids stood up he thought they had misunderstood him, so he had them all sit down. He was so nervous he barely knew what he was saying, but he did his best to explain the story again. Again they stood up — nearly three hundred kids. The meeting ended at half past nine, and from then until almost past midnight kids stood in lines twenty deep, waiting to pray with someone to receive Christ. Eventually we dragged the church deacons out of their Wednesday night meeting to help pray with the kids. What, we wondered, could they possibly be doing that was more important than this?" (p. 40).

9. At the time Bilezikian was teaching at Trinity Evangelical Divinity School. He then moved on to teach at Wheaton College.

10. Hybels and Hybels, *Rediscovering Church*, p. 167.

11. For our purposes the most important text is Gilbert Bilezikian, *Community 101* (Grand Rapids: Zondervan, 1997). Bilezikian, *Christianity 101* (Grand Rapids: Zondervan, 1993), especially chapter 7, which lays out his doctrine of the church, is also pertinent.

Moreover, while it is obvious that Bilezikian does not deploy the language of Schmemann, there is affinity in substance initially. He is deeply concerned at the lack of community in the contemporary church. Indeed, the search for authentic community is front and center in Bilezikian's vision for the future. He plainly thinks that he touches a nerve that many contemporary Christians will readily recognize:

> Lay people and clergy alike express dissatisfaction with churches conducting their business as if they were a business. They compare the stilted and stultifying routines of their church life to the effervescent explosion of Holy Spirit-generated vitality that enabled the church of Pentecost to conquer the ancient world for Christ. They wonder with nostalgia where the power has gone. They realize that they often become lost in a jungle-growth of unbiblical traditions that choke the life out of their churches and stifle their ministries. They yearn to discover the biblical tradition that preceded their various ecclesiastical traditions. They demand a radical return to the basics of biblical teachings about the church as community.[12]

Bilezikian sounds here like a conventional evangelical Protestant who sets his course by Scripture. This is a correct reading of his epistemology of theology.[13] What sets him apart is the overall reading he provides of Scripture. In fact he takes the conventional drama of the Trinity — creation, fall, incarnation, and redemption — and rewrites it with a focus on intimacy and community as the heartbeat of his ontology. He captures this nicely in the slogan: "Only community is forever."[14] Thus the Trinity is the original community of oneness; God's gift to humanity in creation is oneness; the

---

12. Bilezikian, *Christianity 101*, pp. 11-12.

13. This aspect of his thinking is very clear in his catechetical work, *Christianity 101*, chapter 1. It is underscored again and again in his work. Consider: ". . . it behooves Christians to draw, not from their own experiences or tradition but from Scripture, accurate definitions of their communal practices under the microscope of God's Word in order to test its biblical nature, to eliminate ruthlessly traditional accretions that hinder true community, and to replace them with elements of authentic community, biblically defined." Bilezikian, *Christianity 101*, p. 44.

14. This is the title of the first chapter of *Community 101*. See p. 15.

fall involves a rupture of oneness and the onset of alienation; the call of Abram and the creation of the people of Israel is the unshakeable foundation for the building of God's new community in the midst of the forces of anti-community; the coming of the redeemer, Jesus Christ, and his work on the cross is the centerpiece and agency of our oneness with God and with each other; our end now is to be an integral member of God's new community; our ultimate destiny will take the form of "one mass migration from this world to the next";[15] there we will inhabit the heavenly city built and indwelt by God. It follows that community is God's dearest creation and that "the making of community cannot be a side issue or an optional matter for Christians. It is as important to God as one's individual salvation. Without community, there is no Christianity."[16]

Unfortunately, over time the church caved in to the attack on community and rather than being the solution to the quest for community in families, neighborhoods, and nations, she herself has become sick and in need of healing. "Whereas the essential definition of the church is to be the community of oneness that united God's people into one body, the church, after twenty centuries of existence, has to rediscover its own basic identity as community."[17] While the church began well and sustained its proper identity for the early centuries, things began to deteriorate in the fourth century with the alleged conversion of Constantine. Made the official religion of the state, the church turned imperial and institutional. In the Middle Ages, she became an authoritarian organization ruled by clergy who grudgingly dispensed salvation to the faithful. Neither the Reformation with its stress on the right of private interpretation, nor the Enlightenment with its deification of reason, fixed the problem. On the contrary, these tidal waves of change fragmented the church to the point where every individual acts like a church into himself or herself. In reaction to this frenzied fragmentation, others take refuge in massive totalitarianism. Clearly, the way out of this predicament is to return to the Bible and to the vision of oneness to be found there.

Implementing this vision cannot happen without small groups:

15. Bilezikian, *Christianity 101*, p. 38.
16. Bilezikian, *Christianity 101*, p. 35.
17. Bilezikian, *Christianity 101*, p. 48.

For contemporary Christians to meet regularly in small groups is not an option or a luxury. It is a biblical mandate that they must obey if they want to experience communal life and if their churches are to become biblically functioning communities. Whenever church leadership is slow or reluctant to get a small group structure in place as a regular part of its program, lay people have every right to get together and form their own small groups.[18]

Equally important is a social vision of sanctification:

A faulty understanding of sanctification as a self-absorbed, private exercise of personal improvement has a fragmenting effect on the church. It must be replaced with a vigorous, holistic doctrine of sanctification that defines it also as a God-given spiritual cement that makes oneness possible.[19]

Clearly, it is hard to see how either these practices or teachings can be introduced into a local congregation or sustained there without intentional planning and implementation. Indeed the cultivation of a God-designed community requires forethought, organization, coordination, and cooperation. In fact, according to Scripture, "all the work that building community requires is called ministry."[20] The primary form that ministry takes is that of an every-member ministry in which the Holy Spirit equips and empowers each believer. This equipping of every church member is so important that "it should be the responsibility of every church to present a clear teaching about spiritual gifts so that its members have opportunity to discover, develop, and deploy their gifting and thus participate in the ministries of the church."[21] Here is how Bilezikian sums up this vital element of his vision of the church:

18. Bilezikian, *Christianity 101*, pp. 55-56.
19. Bilezikian, *Christianity 101*, pp. 62-63.
20. Bilezikian, *Christianity 101*, p. 65.
21. Bilezikian, *Christianity 101*, p. 80. Compare this very strong claim: "The New Testament definition of ministry requires nothing less than the full participation as co-servants of all the members of a congregation in carrying out the work of the church on the basis of each individual's spiritual gift(s)" (p. 81).

... a consistent pattern may be thus traced from the books of Acts through the letters of the New Testament. The church is described as a community of love and oneness. A normal expression of this oneness is unrestricted involvement of all believers in the ministry of the community. Since this ministry is carried out with each individual contributing his or her spiritual gift, the expectation is for all to use their gifts to the fullest. Instructions that would impede or curtail anyone's participation in church ministry on the basis of race, class, or gender are present neither in the letters surveyed above nor in any other document of the New Testament. . . . Evidently, God is an equal opportunity employer.[22]

This development in the early church represents a new paradigm of community compared to that given in the Old Testament times. Then God tolerated the ministry of priests, prophets, and kings. Now all become priests, for every member is a minister, and all become prophets, for all share in the work of spreading the Word of God. As to kings, there are no longer any kings in God's new community. Because Christ is Lord, the church does not need an earthly ruler; "The Lord in heaven is perfectly capable of managing the affairs of his church on earth, especially since the Holy Spirit is now on location to attend to it."[23]

What if any is the place of leaders in this scheme of things? For Bilezikian, they are clearly important, yet entirely secondary:

Whatever leadership structures existed in the early churches, they were inconspicuous, discreet, self-effacing, and flexible. They seem to have adapted their activities and visibility to local circumstances and needs. Clearly evident is a concern not to preempt congregational initiative and involvement. The leadership of the New Testament churches seems to stand on the sidelines, ready to intervene only in situations of necessity. They are invisible servants, whose role is to equip the body.[24]

22. Bilezikian, *Christianity 101*, p. 90.
23. Bilezikian, *Christianity 101*, p. 73.
24. Bilezikian, *Christianity 101*, p. 97.

The task of such leaders is to facilitate and manage the work of local congregations by operating as servant leaders, by implementing consensual decision making, and by working together in teams.[25] The church as a whole puts in place systems of spiritual watchcare and church discipline. Good leaders will constantly seek to decentralize the work of the church, using all the information and insight they can glean from Scripture and prudent sense.[26] They will also put in place mechanisms to train all members in their personal ministries. In our current situation, good leaders will also ensure that local churches hold effective seeker services that fit with the practice of relational evangelism:

> . . . in true servant form, the local church should make available a periodic and carefully crafted seeker event that is appropriately customized to be intelligible to interested unbelievers, so as to expose them to the life of Christian community and to awaken them to the realization of their need for the gospel. As a result, conversions to Christ and transformed lives become predictable and recurring realities. Seekers become believers, they are integrated in the life of the church, and, in turn, they act as servant messengers with their acquaintances, relatives, friends, co-workers, and neighbors.[27]

For a Biblicist like Bilezikian, this vision does not immediately fit with the choice of twelve male apostles on the part of Jesus. Nor does it fit with the instructions to establish deacons and overseers that are so central in the Pastoral Epistles. In both cases, Bilezikian deploys the same theological explanation. These moves on the part of Jesus and Paul represent an accommodation to the circumstances of their situation. They are appropriate strategic measures that are needed in the short-term, but they do not constitute the normative model of ministry presented in Acts

25. Bilezikian proposes a "New Testament definition of leadership" as follows: "Leadership is a servant ministry, based on spiritual gifts and always plural." Bilezikian, *Christianity 101*, p. 130.

26. Bilezikian does not stress the importance of studies of, say, management, but it is clear that they are not far from the surface. He has initiated a whole raft of literature that mines and deploys this kind of material in an effort to fix the church.

27. Bilezikian, *Christianity 101*, p. 148.

and the Epistles of the New Testament as a whole. Thus Jesus had no choice but to operate with twelve male apostles in his earthly ministry among the Jews; once the worldwide ministry was launched at Pentecost, this provisional accommodation fell by the wayside. As for Paul, in the Pastoral Epistles he was dealing with local congregations that had regressed into infancy and had become threatened with apostasy. For these great ills, strong, short-term remedies were essential. Thereafter the normative pattern of New Testament ministry needed to be reintroduced. This normative pattern is clear in the New Testament:

> The biblical test of true community is very practical. The body is a unit; though it is made of many parts, it functions as one body. The body is complete and healthy when each part functions optimally, in harmony with the other parts. The mark of authentic community is full participation of its members in the ministry of the community. Oneness cannot happen when parts of the body are paralyzed into inaction by ugly discrimination. The atrophy or impairment of part of the body can cripple the whole body (1 Cor. 12:26). But oneness blooms with full effervescence in the heat of joyful and generous teamwork when each part of the body pours out all that is into the building and expansion of community. Then community can become what God intends it to be — not a crippled body but "a radiant church, without stain or wrinkle or any other blemish, but holy and blameless" (Eph. 5:27).[28]

Once we put this vision in place, it is obvious that all is not well in most contemporary forms of the church. Not surprisingly, Bilezikian traces a massive falling away from the normative model he favors. Wrong conceptions and practices of ordination that fostered an aura of pseudo-sanctity, forms of patriarchy and hierarchy that excluded women, and a drive to centralize that undermined the equipping role of leaders, combined to create a sick church. Centralization signals how far we have departed from the normative model that should be in place.

28. Bilezikian, *Christianity 101*, p. 128.

This is the issue on which clear scriptural directives and widely accepted ecclesiastical traditions collide head-on. Amazingly, tradition wins out over Scripture. The change from congregation-based ministries to the emergence of the "minister" as the performer of ministry for the local church did not occur overnight. It was the result of a long, historical process that began in postapostolic times, reached its full development in the medieval church, and was left essentially unchallenged by the Protestant Reformation.[29]

The way out of this dilemma is a gradualist one: church leaders should now initiate such steps as will move the church's life and practice away from the kind of remedial model that is legitimate as a short-term strategy and return her to the proper vision of community presented in Scripture.

Gradually, without stress and trauma, the most restive and entrenched congregation can be changed under the quiet impact of the Holy Spirit. One planted seed can result in unpredictable growth that will cause a dead congregation to be transformed into a thriving, outreaching, radiating center of Christian love. *Ecclesia reformata semper reformanda.* The church that has been reformed needs always to be reformed. Authentic revival is always a revival of community life.[30]

Should this prove daunting, a wealth of literature is available, and "experienced consultants are also available to advise traditional, authority-bound churches about making the transition to communal and participatory forms of congregational life."[31]

We can now make fully explicit the problem-solution schema proposed by Bilezikian. The church has fallen from its original state as God's new community that reflects the oneness of mutuality and equity at the heart of the Trinity. That is the problem. The solution is this: we should now implement the congregationalist vision of mutuality and freedom,

29. Bilezikian, *Christianity 101*, p. 155.
30. Bilezikian, *Christianity 101*, p. 183.
31. Bilezikian, *Christianity 101*, p. 183.

of gifts and service, that has been given to us in the New Testament, but that was lost in the fourth century. Compare this with the problem-solution schema provided by Schmemann, in which the church has lost its sense of ecclesial consciousness in and around the Eucharist. Now a web of secondary consequences has emerged that can only be solved when this crisis is faced. So the primary problem is the loss of ecclesial consciousness in worship. The solution is to return to the ancient and normative practices of the eucharistic liturgy. Once we ascend afresh into the kingdom of God at the table of the Lord, the other problems will find their own ready solution. What they share is the presenting problem, namely, the practice of liturgy. They also share a passion for authentic community. Beyond that we are peering into two radically different worlds.

We must not move too quickly to build bridges between them, were that in fact possible. In good time, we will show how they might be reconciled in a deeper vision of renewal. For now, it is enough to make three observations.

First, it is clear that we can ask too much from the liturgy. The beauty and spiritual riches of, say, the Divine Liturgy of John Chrysostom needs no articulation and defense; those who have been exposed to it will know immediately its treasures. However, the splendid canonical liturgies of the church succeed in part where there has been sufficient spiritual formation to use them intelligently and fully. The liturgy indeed gives access to the holy of holies, but it yields its treasures to those who have been adequately prepared in faith. Moreover, it is the pure in heart who see God, so that without spiritual discernment the reception of the liturgy is bound to be minimal. Schmemann either ignores or neglects the crucial place of Christian initiation and catechesis in preparing for appropriate participation in the liturgy he so brilliantly depicts.

It is this hard, grinding work of spiritual formation that comes to the fore in the liturgical innovations at Willow Creek Community Church. The passion there is to make the gospel known to first-time seekers. One cannot but be in awe of the efforts made to reach the lost in ways that will be culturally sensitive and effective. The aim is to reach out to potential believers who can barely handle a sign of the cross and who are so preoccupied that they will only come to church if they can slot God into their Sunday routine. Thus we can initially understand why most of the traditional liturgical life of the church is shunted away from Sunday and relocated elsewhere on the weekly calendar at Willow Creek. Yet the price paid for this accommodation to culture is enormous. It displays itself immediately in the de-sanctification of time and the ruination of the first day of the week as the church's agreed time for universal celebration. It is surely ironic that a theology designed to express the oneness of the divine Trinity should end by destroying the common work of liturgy. In this instance liturgy has been sacrificed on the altar of missional pragmatism. Where Schmemann asks too much and expects the uninitiated to grasp what is normally available to those adequately prepared, Bilezikian expects too little and permits new converts to set their own price and constraints in worshipping God. Surely we can find a way in which, with adequate catechesis and formation, even the seeker can come to revel in the common life of the church's liturgy.

Second, we need to be frank in naming the ecclesiology represented by Bilezikian. It is old-fashioned, unreconstructed congregationalism. It is amazing that someone so committed to oneness should limit the unity of the church as a whole to that found in the local congregation. Equally, it is extraordinary that a scholar with Bilezikian's training should expect us to see this as "biblical." It is nothing of the sort. On the contrary, it is one more effort to ask Scripture to provide a blueprint for the life of the church. No such blueprint is available. Bilezikian's constant efforts to come up with "biblical" definitions of contested ideas like leadership and ministry are simply farfetched and unconvincing. His attempts to dispose of the choice of the Twelve as a mere missional strategy to Jews on the part of Jesus and to explain away the natural historical developments that shine through the Pastoral Epistles are unpersuasive. These rationalizations display precisely the accommodation to contemporary modes of thought that he himself readily uses to dismiss the catholic dimensions of Christian history. The crux of the matter is this: it is a sheer impossibility for the early church to have followed normative New Testament patterns of ministry when the New Testament did not itself exist. According to Bilezikian's premises, the history of the church up until the fourth century must have been a continuous miracle. The church had to develop its ecclesiology by working up arguments and practices from a canon of texts that as yet did not exist. We need a better way to think about both the history and nature of the church in those formative centuries. If we fail to do so and simply welcome this Trojan horse into our midst, we will wake up some day and find ourselves saddled with a congregationalism that will reproduce precisely the fragmentation that Bilezikian rightly excoriates. On the other hand, if we pay attention to the fullness of Schmemann's vision of the church, we may find a second Trojan horse has landed on our shores. If that is the case, we will have to be doubly careful in our judgments.

Third, this in no way means we can dismiss or ignore what is happening in experiments like Willow Creek. Happily, the Holy Spirit does not ask permission from the Eastern Orthodox bishops, or even from the Pope in Rome, when she is reaching out to disoriented and confused souls in search of liberation and healing. Happily, the Son's work of redemption is available even in those accommodated liturgies and ecclesial practices that can all too readily collapse into vulgar entertainment and secular achievements. Happily, the Father is out on the prowl looking for lost sheep, and when those he has historically and publicly appointed to find them and bring them home themselves get lost, he is well able to find others who will shoulder the burdens involved. Any comprehensive vision of renewal must find a way to accommodate the extraordinary as well as the ordinary work of the blessed Trinity.

CHAPTER 7

POSTMODERNITY, OR DEATH BY ONE'S OWN HAND

DON CUPITT AND EDWARD NORMAN

IT IS COMMONPLACE TO OBSERVE that, culturally speaking, we are now well into a massive transition from modernity to postmodernity. Given the deep connections that exist between the church and her host cultures, it would be astonishing if the relation between the gospel and postmodernity did not surface in proposals about renewal. This is precisely what we find. However, the discerning observer is faced with a dilemma at this point. Postmodernity comes in a variety of forms. Most saliently, it shows up in a popular and vulgar form, but it shows up in more sophisticated versions as well. It can also show up in a right-wing or left-wing variety. Advocates of the former accept the fundamental orientation of postmodernity as an analysis of contemporary culture but argue that it involves a drive to nihilism and violence; hence it can only be overcome by a retrieval of "radical orthodoxy" as represented by Augustine.[1] The left-wing postmodernists welcome the appearance of postmodernity, if need be embracing the nihilism it unleashes. Moreover, some who tackle the relation between the gospel and contemporary culture prefer to speak generically, folding the debate about postmodernity into a wider discussion.

---

1. This is a position now especially associated with John Milbank, Catherine Pickstock, Graham Ward, and others, and made known in a variety of lively but very dense texts. See for example, John Milbank, *Theology and Social Theory: Beyond Secular Reason* (Oxford: Blackwell, 1990).

It would be tempting to turn aside and explore the wider issues entailed by such moves in detail, but that would be a distraction. Our strategy in exploring renewal has been simpler and more effective. We have stuck closely to the singularity of what particular activists or theologians have offered. There is no need to make an exception in this chapter, where again we shall allow the renewalists under review to speak on their own terms. We turn to two Anglican theologians in England who represent profoundly opposing positions: Don Cupitt [1934-] and Edward Norman [1938-]. We begin with the more famous of the two.

Don Cupitt began life as an orthodox believer[2] but has become the poster child of postmodern Christianity in England. Over an academic career that has resulted in the publication of over thirty books and in the presentation of a popular television documentary on the loss of faith in the modern period, he has distanced himself more and more from his early orthodoxy. He is also the founder of a network known as the Sea of Faith.[3] As fellow of Emmanuel College, Cambridge, he has taught philosophy of religion there for most of his academic career. As a writer Cupitt operates at times less as an analytical philosopher and more like a musician who takes up a series of melodies and constantly returns to them in different keys.[4] This is especially so in his *Reforming Christianity,* a recent summary of his proposals on the renewal of Christianity for a new age.

The image of the sea of faith is as good a place as any from where to begin. Cupitt borrows it from the famous poem by Matthew Arnold in the late nineteenth century, entitled "Dover Beach." The image is a powerful one that conjures up the loss of belief that has become a marked feature of English society over the last century and a half. After a descrip-

---

2. This is made clear in Stephen Ross White, *Don Cupitt and the Future of Christian Doctrine* (London: SCM, 1994).

3. The title comes from a television series that bore the title "Sea of Faith." A book from the same series, written by Cupitt and with the same title, has also appeared. Those in the network have resisted seeing themselves as a movement because to do so would be to provide a determinate content that they intentionally eschew. Information under the name "Sea of Faith" is available on the Internet.

4. Cupitt's style strikes one initially as repetitive. Characteristically he provides a kind of spiraling argument and narrative so that with each repetition the theme is enriched and extended. This point is well made by Arthur J. Dewey in his Foreword to Cupitt, *Reforming Christianity* (Santa Rosa, Calif.: Poleridge Press, 2001), p. xii.

tion of the sea throwing up pebbles on the beach, the pertinent stanzas from Arnold run:

> The Sea of Faith
> Was once, too, at the full, and round earth's shore
> Lay like the folds of a bright girdle furl'd.
> But now I can only hear
> Its melancholy, long, withdrawing roar,
> Retreating, to the breath
> Of the night-wind, down the vast edges drear
> And naked shingles of the world.
>
> Ah, Love, let us be true
> To one another! For the world, which seems
> To lie before us like a land of dreams,
> So various, so beautiful, so new,
> Hath really neither joy, nor love, nor light,
> Nor certitude, nor peace, nor help for pain;
> And we are here as on a darkling plain
> Swept with confused alarms of struggle and flight,
> Where ignorant armies clash by night.

Cupitt departs from Arnold in that he has no nostalgia for the established ways of state and religion in England that were so dear to Arnold. Cupitt is, in fact, a scathing critic of the Anglican establishment. Arnold foresaw the massive decline in Christianity, and appears, at least in this poem, to have sought solace and escape in the joys of personal loyalty and love. Cupitt documents the decline, but he has no regrets about the passing of established Christianity. Thus he points out that in England, the church declines by twenty-five percent every ten years; over a generation, the numbers are halved. Clearly Arnold would not be happy with this forlorn confirmation of his poetic prediction. Cupitt, however, takes it in stride. For him it is the unfolding of a historical drama, which needs to be understood and welcomed on its own terms. This historical drama is at the core of his vision of renewal, for in an interesting way Cupitt is at heart a theological dispensationalist who revels in the arrival of a wholly secular culture.

Again and again, he returns to this historical drama, whose central narrative runs like this. Current institutional or official Christianity is in decline, but this simply means the end of ecclesiastical Christianity; it does not mean the end of the message of Jesus or the religion he inaugurated in his message of the kingdom of God. From the beginning the life and work of Jesus was overlaid with a network of Scripture, creeds, rituals, and priests who displaced the kingdom and instituted a system of mediation that got in the way of the kingdom. There were in fact two groups among the followers of Jesus, a kingdom group and a church group:

> The "Kingdom" people were more quakerish or existentialist in outlook: they wanted to continue to live in the Kingdom way and they "heard" the sayings of Jesus as confirming their point of view. But the "Church" party, closer to Paul, were conscious that the Kingdom had not fully come. In the waiting period it was necessary to come to some sort of accommodation with the old, violent social order and its institutions. People of this turn of mind, who urged reflection and calculation, also "heard" the tradition of Jesus' sayings — but they heard it as confirming *their* point of view. So it came about that when all the sayings were collected and written down, they came to include both Kingdom sayings that said *Go the whole hog: be conspicuous,* and the Church sayings that said *Work quietly and unobtrusively, like the yeast in the dough.*[5]

The church party won out in the struggle between these two groups, and Cupitt traces four subsequent stages in the development across the centuries. In stage one, the church wrestled with the delay of the kingdom by positing that Jesus was resurrected from the dead, had moved off stage where he was visible to the eye of faith, and from which he would soon return. In the meantime, the church worshipped him as Lord and

---

5. Cupitt, *Reforming Christianity,* p. 55 (emphasis in the original). As we shall see, Cupitt thinks that Jesus' views were truly reflected in the kingdom group.

called on him to return. In stage two, in the sub-apostolic period, the church developed a complex system of mediated religion, complete with beliefs, sacraments, and a hierarchy who came to reduce the church to themselves and to control every aspect of her life. In stage three the church became an end in itself, claiming to be indefectible and infallible. Its doctrines became a passport to heaven. Life was to be spent preparing for death, as the church dispensed sacramental grace "according to strict rules by a highly bureaucratic salvation machine that processes souls en masse for Heaven."[6] In stage four, that began in the later Middle Ages, a few brave souls challenged the church as an end in herself, but the church refortified herself so that it now became the religious object of faith: "The believer believes in the Pope, the Creed, the Church and the Sacraments: intellectual and moral thralldom to the machine is what gives to ordinary believers their sense of security that they come to think of as being 'faith' and as true religion."[7]

Not surprisingly, on this analysis, dissent broke out on the part of mystics, Protestants, and rebellious theologians. The real breakthrough, however, came in the nineteenth century with Nietzsche's claim that God was dead. From then on, many gave up on some other, supernatural world and turned to the world of our present life. This set the stage for Cupitt's new reformation:

> Against this background I am suggesting that today the reformation of Christianity must proceed by going back to the beginning in order to go forwards. It is necessary to recall the curiously complicated story of the Faith's first origins and early development, in order to see why it is now time to abandon Church theology and push the Christian movement forwards in to the next long promised stage of its historical development: the Kingdom. The Kingdom is purely of this present world: it is a new ethic, and a new relationship to life. It is post-ecclesiastical and post-dogmatic. We've been praying daily for it all these years. Now its time has come.[8]

6. Cupitt, *Reforming Christianity*, p. 7.
7. Cupitt, *Reforming Christianity*, p. 8.
8. Cupitt, *Reforming Christianity*, p. 9.

The kingdom of God has now arrived afresh, emptied out into the secular.[9] God has come so close that he disappears; the religious world now coincides with the life of the world, and everything becomes holy. Following the real Jesus of history, rather than the Christ of faith invented by the early Church, we should live our lives in reckless abandon.[10] We no longer need mediation with some invisible world beyond this world, for the whole drift of modern science, modern scholarship, and biblical study has undermined belief in the supernatural. Modern philosophy from Kant through Hegel, Wittgenstein, and Heidegger makes it clear that we culturally and linguistically create the world we inhabit. The world comes to expression through us and reveals both itself and us as thoroughly transient and contingent. There is no real world or self outside our language and concepts. There is no objective world. There is no truth outside the meeting of language and being. There are no essential substances; there is simply the utterly transient, contingent flow of life; "there is ultimately nothing but an endless dance of phenomena, seemings."[11] If we cannot see this for ourselves, then a brush with death will bring it home to us.[12] Death shows us that we come to be and pass away. In the light of this we should imitate the divine by pouring ourselves into life with gusto and abandon.[13]

9. Cupitt sees the secular as represented here by the secularist traditions of the United States of America and of the state of Israel: "I have argued that we should recognize in this new and increasingly globalized Western culture a secular fulfillment of the Christian hope. If we can show this new culture its own history and its own religious significance, and if within it we can pioneer new religious values and lifestyles, then we will indeed gradually 'build Jerusalem' and turn it all into as full a realization of religious hope as there can be." See Cupitt, *Reforming Christianity*, p. 81. The problem, as Cupitt sees it, is that religious conservatives keep showing up to attack and disrupt this eschatology.

10. For Cupitt this process of invention began with the gospel of John.

11. Cupitt, *Reforming Christianity*, p. 23. Cupitt repeatedly draws attention to the affinities between his position and that of Madhyamika or Middle-Way Buddhism. He is also careful to mark one crucial difference: "From the point of view of Kingdom religion Buddhism seems a little too unattached, cool and celibate. The Buddha is wise and compassionate: he does not experience suffering. Christ is furiously ardent: he loves and suffers greatly. Who do we choose to follow? It's up to you." Cupitt, *Reforming Christianity*, p. 58.

12. Cupitt had several close calls in 1992.

13. This might suggest that, as related to the topic of marriage, we are "learning to use sex as being simply the best and richest form of interpersonal exchange." Cupitt turns sur-

Cupitt's own favored way of describing the contrast between the church and the kingdom comes in a kind of checklist:

First, in ecclesiastical theology the whole world of the here and now is subordinated to a greater and better World Beyond, whereas in kingdom theology there is no beyond at all. All is arrival, victory, and rest in the here and now.

Most of the other contrasts are related to the first one. Thus, and *secondly,* in ecclesiastical religion God is transcendent, Other, and unknown, whereas in the kingdom God is wholly immanent. *Thirdly,* ecclesiastical religion is mediated by authoritative scriptures, creeds, rituals and priests, whereas kingdom religion is immediate and intuitive. *Fourthly,* in ecclesiastical religion, dogmatic faith is *sine qua non,* whereas kingdom religion is visionary and beliefless. There being no unseen beyond, dogmatic faith is not needed. The reason why one lives *after belief* is the same reason why one lives *after history:* one is no longer aspiring after or waiting for anything unseen that one does not already have. *Fifthly,* in ecclesiastical theology there is much emphasis on rank, hierarchy and inequalities, whereas kingdom theology is highly egalitarian and knows nothing of titles or degrees of rank. Ecclesiastical religion is popish, and kingdom theology is quakerish. *Sixthly,* ecclesiastical theology canonizes one particular vocabulary, a particular cultural tradition and particular lineages of teaching authority, whereas kingdom theology has forgotten tradition and is at last fully "ecumenical" or globalized — i.e. catholic or panethnic.

Generalizing, and *seventhly,* one may say that in the ecclesiastical world great importance is attached to the fact that much is mysterious, dark, latent, unseen and generally beyond our ken, whereas in the kingdom everything is explicit, out in the open, equally lit and plain, with no darkness or shadows at all. People are entirely transparent to each other. So also and *eighthly,* whereas the ecclesiastical world is a

---

prisingly conservative at this point. "In the kingdom, one possible form of Free Love is that which decides to keep choosing and winning the same partner afresh each day." See Cupitt, *Reforming Christianity,* p. 82.

world of many languages, of pluralism and discord, the kingdom world is a world of one equal music. And *finally*, in ecclesiastical culture a clear and very important distinction is made between the sacred and profane realms, whereas in the kingdom the sacred/profane distinction is simply not made. Or we may say if we wish that the common speech of plain people is itself the only sacred language.[14]

Two questions naturally occur to the observer at this point. First, how does this vision relate to the proposals of Bishop John Shelby Spong that we examined in an earlier chapter? While there are clear affinities between the two,[15] Cupitt is insistent that there are very significant differences. To begin, he thinks that Spong provides one more version of the liberal Protestantism that has failed again and again to make a difference in the church. The various forms of orthodoxy have constantly found a way to marginalize and keep the kind of revisionist proposals developed by Spong at bay.[16] Further, he is convinced that Spong's attempt to translate the faith into the language of the contemporary world is "woolly and vague. The old, cruel, hard edged vocabulary always seems clearer and more definite than the gentler vocabulary that the liberals are trying to put in its place."[17] Neither of these observations are surprising, he suggests, if we recall that Spong is a bishop of the church, hopelessly constrained by his office to make utterances that mean one thing to one section of his audience and another thing to another. "In the short term he may gain notoriety and goodish sales figures, but his long-term political failure is certain because of the way the group dynamics of the church operate."[18]

14. Cupitt, *Reforming Christianity*, pp. 33-34 (emphasis in the original). This is a quotation from one of Cupitt's earlier books that is repeated here and thus clearly marks out his own summary analysis.

15. Both acknowledge, for example, a massive debt to the work of Bishop John Robinson in the 1960s.

16. After a catalogue of revisionist writers and books that have failed to carry the day, Cupitt remarks, "People have learnt nothing and remembered nothing. Liberal theology has made no progress and achieved nothing." See Cupitt, *Reforming Christianity*, p. 76. Earlier he wistfully comments, "We may detest Augustine and Calvin, but we really cannot equal them" (p. 72).

17. Cupitt, *Reforming Christianity*, p. 69.

18. Cupitt, *Reforming Christianity*, p. 71.

The second question follows naturally: Why then bother with the church at all? If it is so hopelessly stuck in a time warp, why continue to hold office or receive its sacraments? First, because like in an art gallery, innovations are more readily understood and recognized when they are framed against the traditional alternative: ". . . it is very convenient to use the church and her language as a 'shell company', or a convenient backdrop against which we can explain kingdom religion and show up what is novel and distinctive about it."[19] Second, postmodernist renewalists should stay in the church because the new vision developed as kingdom theology is mined from within the church's founder teaching as mediated by her scriptures.[20] Thus the resources for change come from within the church herself. Finally, the church provides the theater for rediscovering real Christianity:

> . . . the Church is still the necessary theatre; partly because the church is still the best public space or theatre in which to proclaim and test out new initiatives in lifestyle and spirituality; and partly because the church, despite itself, still carries deeply buried in its memory the necessary concepts for explaining and interpreting the Kingdom religion. That the Church is still the best available frame and theatre is recognized by all those people who use it and borrow its vocabulary in order to propagate their Liberation theology, feminist theology, black theology, green theology, black feminist theology, and so on. Lesbigays do not scruple to use the church — or what is left of it — as a useful theatre and proving ground in which to pursue the cause of social emancipation of sexual minorities: and I think they are right. After all, the various causes named — the emancipation of the poor, of women, of minority races, of sexual minorities, and of the earth itself — these are all good kingdom causes. So why should we also not take encouragement from them, and pursue the ultimate unscrupulousness of using the church as an arena in which to attempt to try and propagate even *Christianity?*[21]

19. Cupitt, *Reforming Christianity*, p. 129.
20. Cupitt clearly operates with a canon within the canon at this point.
21. Cupitt, *Reforming Christianity*, p. 86.

How should we summarize Cupitt's diagnosis of the church's current slide into decline? Decline arises because the church is wedded to a form of dogmatic theology that betrays the message of the kingdom and that in turn is tied to an objectivist, realist reading of its own language. This theology and its practices has become traditionalist, authoritarian, intellectually dishonest, uncritical, idolatrous, oppressive, and out of step with contemporary culture. The prescription is straightforward. The church should rediscover the kingdom message of the historical Jesus, come to terms with the evolving emptying out of the divine into secular and profane culture, abandon her self-serving realist and essentialist metaphysics, and live out an affirmation of life in the face of the inescapable reality of death.

Cupitt's vision of the history, nature, and renewal of the church is clearly provocative. He gives the impression that he is simply describing what is actually happening across the sweep of the church's history. He writes as if he is just unfolding a narrative of history whose natural end is his vision of contemporary Western culture. One only has to survey the literature on modernity and postmodernity to know that there are radically different historical and normative readings of the same terrain. One theologian and historian who takes an entirely different view of that terrain is another prolific Anglican scholar, Edward Norman,[22] who has supplied a wonderfully lucid account of his own views in his book, *Secularisation*.[23] Like Cupitt, he takes the fact of massive decline of the church in England as his starting point. However, he provides a very different diagnosis as to what has gone wrong and a radically different prescription as to how to put things right. To these we now turn.

The best way into Norman's position is by noting his description of the radical shift between the England of the eighteenth century and England today. In the England of the long eighteenth century, there was a confessional state, an established and confessional church, and a broadly Christian culture. Now we have a secular state, a secular culture, and the mere remnants of an established church. This story of how edu-

---

22. Like Cupitt, Norman's academic roots are in Cambridge, and like Norman he has been a very successful broadcaster.

23. Norman, *Secularisation* (London: Continuum, 2002).

cation, parliament, legislation, the media, and the culture gradually shed its Christian character and aspirations is too well known to need repeating here. We should note three things in Norman's general analysis that set his reading of the history apart from most others. First, we should not take the evaluation of the culture's current exponents and apologists at face value. Thus, while there is much talk of pluralism, relativism, and freedom, in reality the state has not at all ceased to be confessional. On the contrary, the culture is much more monolithic than it pretends, and the state is relentless in pressing its own ideology and values into legislation and in the culture as a whole.[24] Second, the new culture, while it may have its merits here and there, is not all it is cracked up to be; it lacks depth, it promises illusory emancipation, it is devoted to conspicuous consumption, it sanitizes and avoids the harsh realities of life, it is incurably and imprudently romantic, and it constantly ministers to human vanity.[25] Third, far from being the embodiment of the kingdom of God, it is utterly incompatible with the Christian faith. It is in fact the embodiment of a soft and creeping version of secular humanism. This whole way of thinking and acting stands in sharp contrast to the message of Christ.

> The message proclaimed by Christ was about the corruption and sinfulness of men and women, their inability to procure their own redemption, and the forgiveness which he held out to those who repented. It was about an intrinsic bias to evil in human nature which could not be eradicated but whose lamentable consequences could be forgiven. Humanism, in contrast, declares an optimistic view of the capabilities of men and women: they are entitled to moral autonomy, achieve progressive improvement in the conditions of life on earth, are broadly able to control the human aspects of development, and

24. "Universal education, electronic communication (especially television), the computer revolution, the rise of new and articulate social myths, have dispatched effective diversity: a single culture, existing in different levels and reflecting the survival of class consciousness, has come to inhabit both rural and urban, the more and the less socially homogenous." Norman, *Secularisation*, p. 113.

25. The title of another of Norman's books is self-revealing: *Entering the Darkness: Christianity and Its Modern Substitutes* (London: SPCK, 1991).

are known to possess rights which dignify the individual without the need for reference to any transcendent authority.[26]

The obvious question facing the church in this transition is: How has she dealt with this competing vision of the order of things? In recording Norman's reply to this question we come close to his diagnosis for our present woes. The leadership of the church has systematically and intentionally embraced the enemy within its own borders. The leaders have aided and abetted the internal secularization of the church's life from top to bottom:

> . . . the main reason for the velocity with which the Church is in decline derives from its own internal secularization, from its voluntary and largely unconscious adoption of the ideas and practices of the benign adversaries who came to it with friendly countenances and largely innocent intentions. . . . Christianity is not being rejected in modern society — what is causing the decline of the public support for the Church is the insistence of its own leaders in representing secular enthusiasm for humanity as core Christianity. In one sense the Church has as little to declare that is distinctive in a society that is hard put to turn out for a football match, let alone a religious service. Institutional Christianity has lost the capacity to influence the culture on the one hand, and the culture is progressively secularized on the other.
>
> The Church could, in another arrangement of things, have withstood the secularization of the culture. It is not that secularization as such which has felled it, but the adoption of the Church of secular thought — death by one's own hand.[27]

Norman proceeds to document this charge in a freewheeling review of the church's educational institutions and norms, her general culture,

---

26. Norman, *Secularisation*, p. 1.

27. Norman, *Secularisation*, p. ix. Elsewhere Norman makes the same point forcefully this way. "Christianity has not really suffered at the hands of intellectual enlightenment; there has been, indeed, very little inclination to assail it. The enemy was within, dismantling the walls of the building with all the best intentions and with the zeal of converts." Norman, *Secularisation*, p. 153.

the use of church buildings, her relations with the state and politics, the content and sources of her moral teaching, her systematic and moral theological reflection, her rite and rituals, her worship, and her philosophy of priesthood and ministry. Three examples will suffice to make his position clear.

First, take the issue of church schools. Given its official convictions about pluralism and relativism, the state, of course, has abandoned the idea that the state schools should privilege the Christian faith:

> What needs to be explained is how the leaders of Church apply the same judgments of educational intention in the schools conducted under their auspices, and which were founded explicitly to teach Christianity. For despite some notable exceptions, the schools run by the Church, both secondary and primary, follow precisely the same practices in relation to religion as do the state schools.[28]

We find the same neutral hiring policies, the same refusal to teach Christian doctrine, the same religious relativism, and the same effort to indoctrinate on issues of gender, race, and social distribution. Clearly, the leadership of the church has lost its intellectual nerve. It should come, then, as no surprise that many believing Christians do not know the faith to which they formally assent.[29]

Second, consider the use of church buildings — for example, the great cathedrals. Cathedrals are extremely expensive to maintain, hence the need to appeal to the state for money for upkeep and hence the readiness to open the cathedrals to the tourist industry or to the more elite end of the music market. Naturally church leaders justify this move on religious grounds. They go along because these great cultural representations are one way of conveying the Christian faith. But to move in this direction is to give the store away:

---

28. Norman, *Secularisation*, p. 14.

29. Norman holds out little hope for Sunday schools providing the necessary antidote to the general trends in education. He has provided a fascinating short book for interested seekers entitled *An Anglican Catechism* (London: Continuum, 2001).

Behind this lies the assumption, so widespread with the intelligentsia of the times, that science and modern knowledge are all about reality, and that religion is all about the emotions; and that objective truth is to be sought entirely in the realm of material explanation, and that religious "experience" resides in personal sensation and aesthetic appreciation; that the real data about the nature of things, so to say, excludes the "poetic" faculties which are catered for by religious belief. Authentic Christianity, in complete contrast, is centered in doctrinal truths which are known through the transmission of a living company of adherents, and is in no sense dependent upon the emotional condition of the individual. Christ did not talk about aesthetic experiences but about sin, repentance, and redemption. His body in the world, the Church, has for two millennia found that a knowledge of these things needs to be taught directly to the people — it is only in our own day that we have come to regard art history or past folk perceptions of faith to be the most appropriate method.[30]

Third, consider what has happened in academic theology. To begin, it has long been, and continues to be, in the hands of the liberal wing of the church. The Evangelical wing of the church has not produced the scholarship needed for academic appointment, and the Catholic wing has been too wounded to make a difference on this front. Thus theological education has mostly fallen into the hand of the wrong side in the current divide in the church:

In the English churches of the present day . . . differences of the past, though they persist, are enormously overshadowed by the contrast between those who adhere still to "traditional" interpretations of doctrinal formulae, who understand Christianity as a fixed body of structured teaching, and those "liberal" clerics and thinkers for whom the religious faith has become virtually open-ended exploration of human responses to intimations of a divine purpose in existence.[31]

30. Norman, *Secularisation*, p. 31.
31. Norman, *Secularisation*, p. 62.

Consequently both the methodology and content of theology has been seriously affected. To be sure, intellectual inquiry is vital to the health and communication of the Christian message;

> Interpretation of the data, however, needs to be informed by values which often derive from intellectual attitudes, and traditions of understanding to which religion brings unique insights. When this is left out of comprehension the result is, as in present circumstances, the secularization of analysis and explanation. Sometimes it is simply because the secular modes of intellectual enquiry are inappropriate when applied to the data which derives from Revealed Truth. More commonly, however, theological interpretation proceeds by removing aspects of traditional religious belief — in miraculous phenomena, for example, or in the intrinsic corruption of human nature — which is considered by modern intellectual culture to be implausible or literally incredible.[32]

This narrowing of intellectual vision, in turn, paves the way for the construal of Jesus as a moral teacher of human decencies expressed in the dated vocabulary of mysterious symbolism. More dangerous still, it creates space for the reduction of Christianity to benign views of human nature and to the vision of ethical virtue championed by the bourgeois intelligentsia.[33]

Given a diagnosis that sharply focuses on the failure of leadership, it is not surprising that the prescription for change has a similar shape. Yet nowhere does he suggest that we need a simple return to an earlier golden age of the Church of England. On the contrary, the current crisis in the church makes manifest fault lines that go right back to her initial beginnings. At the outset the Church of England was "a kind of half-rejected di-

---

32. Norman, *Secularisation*, p. 62.

33. Norman repeatedly insists that it is the ethical content of Christianity that provides the critical slipways for the infiltration of alien materials and practices: "Once Christ has been represented as primarily concerned with justice and welfare, rather than sin and corruption, the equation of his religion with the leading tenets of modern Humanism is easily effected." Norman, *Secularisation*, p. 3.

gest of Calvinism made in the sixteenth and seventeenth centuries" that "never really adjusted to match the surviving traditionalism of the Church's organizational structures."[34] This initial incoherence has continued over time. The church is now home to a lethal combination of the rejection of authority and the welcoming of self-selective, do-it-yourself forms of Christianity. "At the center of the problem of secularization, and the reason why its effects on the Church are now so dire, is the coincidence of an imprecise definition of authority within the English Protestant tradition and the modern individualizing of religious choice."[35] The Church of England has no effective means of resisting the process of infiltration that now besets her. Nor does she have the will to do so; she has become a willing partner in her own internal secularization. As a result ". . . there is a kind of stasis; in the increasingly stagnant waters the living creatures move in ever murkier light and feed off the sickly prolific growths."[36] Christianity's "genius for locating human misery in the spiritual frailty of individual humans, which once lay at the heart of its social message, has faded with the ghostly images of a former age."[37] This whole process needs to be arrested in its tracks. Thus what is needed now is a retrieval of a vision of the church as the body of Christ spread out through time and equipped with the authority to identify truth and error.

This vision begins with precisely those elements that are rejected by modern liberal and radical forms of Christianity. We need to re-embrace the robust vision of miraculous revelation that is at the core of the Christian faith:

> . . . without another world to stand upon there is no way in moving this one; without a miraculous intervention in the means by which men and women can know God there can never be any certainty that universal intimations of his presence, and all their cultural reflections, were anything other than the inventions of humanity.[38]

34. Norman, *Secularisation*, p. viii.
35. Norman, *Secularisation*, p. 93.
36. Norman, *Secularisation*, p. 125.
37. Norman, *Secularisation*, p. 40.
38. Norman, *Secularisation*, p. 69.

God has given us the truth in Christ and he has secured that truth in his body, the church. The Church of England needs to take her stand with the church through the ages and develop an authoritative teaching office.

> When a body cannot identify its enemies it gets taken over by them. The body needs immunology. The Church needs an institutional means of determining error — or it will become, as it has already become in some measure, a victim of its own ideological opponents.[39]

How this is to be implanted in the current climate and with the current structures is not entirely clear. Indeed, at one point Norman matter-of-factly points out that any serious attempt at the imposition of unitary teaching in doctrinal matters would result in the collapse of the Church of England.[40] We can, however, tackle the problem by making proper provision for the training of clergy and laity.

For the priesthood such provision stands on the recovery of teaching as at the very center of their vocation:[41] ". . . Christ himself sent out his followers to teach the people, and the truths he declared were exclusive. As sacred employees priests operate solely within the teaching sanctioned by those who employ them."[42] Clearly this kind of vision will mean a radical alteration of the kind of study to which they are introduced.

> Courses of study should be stable and uniform throughout the Church, the curricula in use should be precise and not open-ended, and the students should be conscious that they are being trained to propagate approved interpretation of faith and morals and not their own selections or constructions. This is even more necessary at a time like the present, when the intellectual capacities and educational

39. Norman, *Secularisation*, p. 100.
40. Norman, *Secularisation*, p. 97.
41. Norman by no means limits himself to preparing priests to fulfill their vocation as teachers. His vision of the priesthood embraces a strong personal discipline, a robust sense of identity, and a clear commitment to ecclesiastical obedience.
42. Norman, *Secularisation*, p. 128.

achievements of those coming forward for ordination, are, in relation to the levels general in society, declining. Speculative thought by those who are insufficiently gifted in the attributes of learning will inevitably produce corrosive effects; it will tend, in time, to bring the whole presentation of the Christian religion into intellectual disrepute.[43]

This might appear to sanction a retreat from dealing with the intellectual quest for explanation that is so widespread in the culture. However, this very training is itself part of the answer to this worry.

It is best to go back to fundamentals: if the priests are trained in a clear understanding of authoritative doctrine the explanations they offer to a questioning culture will carry the authority of universal institution. It can stand on its own; it does not require the reformulations by individuals. The Church is the body of Christ in the world: by definition, it cannot speak with more than one voice in its presentation of essential doctrines, and the priests should be trained accordingly.[44]

If this looks like the abandonment of serious scholarship, then we have misread Norman. His answer to this concern is to turn this kind of work over for the most part to laity. Given the past record of distinguished clerical scholarship, this is a regrettable conclusion. However, it is realistic to think along these lines. Moreover, it should be noted that there is in this new development a place for restatement and even reformulation. The doctrines, teachings, and practices of the Church are going to need "progressively more radical re-statement, in circumstances of disintegrating and re-formulating culture."[45] "Christian symbols will have to be rescued from the detritus of a collapsed cultural world, and rendered in the emerging images and symbols of the new."[46] Furthermore, given the

43. Norman, *Secularisation*, p. 129.
44. Norman, *Secularisation*, p. 132.
45. Norman, *Secularisation*, p. 126.
46. Norman, *Secularisation*, p. 96.

continued demise of church colleges, it would help to have at least one good scholarly center to do this kind of work:

> In the winding down of trusts and properties of existing colleges, . . . consideration should be given to the reservation of some of the funds, and one of the properties, for the establishment of an Anglican College of Sacred Learning. What might be envisaged is a small college of priests and qualified laymen, of academic distinction, who should provide what the Church of England now so notably lacks: a resource of higher scholarship, under its own patronage and control, with a clear confessional purpose and centered in a shared devotional life.[47]

We are now in a position to map precisely the proposals on offer. For Norman, the fundamental problem facing the church has been in the arena of the church's leadership. Over time the leaders of the Church of England have quietly and systematically secularized the church from the inside, adopting a seemingly benign humanistic ideology. The bridge to this new and alien world was created out of the secondary elements of the church's life. The bridge was built, that is, out of the church's ethical and humane convictions. The result has been disastrous. Most conspicuously, the church's tough-minded but realistic doctrines have been reduced to a thinned-out version of the Christian faith and then elbowed aside. In capitulating to the intellectual constraints of the day, many church leaders and members have abandoned the rootedness and warrant for doctrine in divine revelation as identified, preserved, and validated by the church as the body of Christ. Negatively, the solution is for the church to recover her intellectual nerve and to back away from the seductive but superficial arguments of the revisionists in her midst. Positively, the church must regain her hold on the truth delivered in the church catholic. Ideally this means the recovery or creation of an authoritative teaching office. More proximately, the church should institute the kind of spiritual and intellectual formation and training that will make the teaching of the truth of

47. Norman, *Secularisation*, p. 147.

Christianity absolutely primary in the work and mission of her leaders. The current situation is one marked by extreme urgency. While the church as the body of Christ will survive, it has died out before in places where it has flourished. Currently, it is not clear if leadership of the church will come to terms with the catastrophe that has befallen the faith. Many fail to appreciate the crisis: "So it must have seemed to the last who lit a votive flame in honour of Apollo, or who celebrated as an initiate of Mithras in the ruins of a collapsed empire."[48]

Turning to look at Cupitt and Norman from a single angle, it is easy to note the differences. Cupitt is an atheist, explicitly using the church as a theater in which to further his own idiosyncratic vision of Jesus. Norman is an Anglo-Catholic, hoping against hope that the Church of England may wake up and take action to restore the substance of catholic identity. Cupitt is at once serene and playful. Norman is at once sober and apocalyptic. Cupitt would appear to represent the forces of open scholarly investigation. Norman looks as if he wants to restrict scholarship drastically. Cupitt would appear to be all for creativity and freedom. Norman looks as if he is counseling passivity and slavish obedience. The polarization is dramatic and profound.

While there is no middle way between these alternatives, we can surely salvage much from both our protagonists.

Surely Norman is right to protest the easy capitulation of church leaders to the internal secularization of the church's life. But surely any prescription must involve much more than the recovery of a teaching office that somehow in itself secures the truth of the faith.

Surely Cupitt is right that there must be a lively and authentically personal appropriation of the faith in any generation that must go beyond passive obedience. But surely his vision of the content of the Christian faith is doomed to a very short shelf life in the academy and in the culture.

Surely Norman is right to insist on the substance of catholic Christianity as mediated in its fullness in the Scriptures, the creeds, and the sacramental life of the church. But surely he is wide of the mark when he

48. Norman, *Secularisation*, p. 154.

reduces the doctrine of the church to a vision of the manner in which Christianity is known to be true, and when he limits her canon of sacred Scripture to a record and set of proofs of the Christian revelation.[49]

Surely Cupitt is right that the church must find a way to enter into the nooks and crannies of modern life and culture. But surely he is wrong to baptize what he finds there as if it cannot be redeemed and transfigured by the action of the living God.

Surely Norman is correct to desire the creation of specifically Anglican centers of scholarship, piety, and worship. But surely he is wrong to deploy the standard caricature of evangelicalism as resting in a purely emotional faith that has nothing to offer contemporary scholarship at its best.

Surely Cupitt is on the right lines in making use of smaller networks and societies to help people find their way in a radically disorienting culture. But surely he is wrong to make these the carriers of material and practice that destroy the canonical faith of the church and operate on policies of dishonesty and dissimulation.

Surely Norman is right to call attention to the great strengths of the Roman Catholic tradition in preserving the faith. But surely he is naive to ignore the full epistemological paraphernalia that have been put in place to make this possible within her borders.

Surely Cupitt is right to focus on the kingdom of God as the very heartbeat of the message of Jesus. But surely he tortures and denies the evidence that connects the kingdom to the actual historical practices, materials, persons, and institutions that clearly emerge from within the circle of Christ's closest disciples.

The challenge ahead will be to find a way to leave behind that which should not be emulated or retained. That can be done relatively easily, that is, by excision and subtraction. The greater challenge will be to integrate the positive elements identified here into a realistic and theologically sensitive vision of the renewal of the church. Again we must resist the temptation for premature closure in moving to that level immediately. There is one more round of contrasts we need to visit.

---

49. This is brought out most clearly in Norman, *Secularisation*, p. 94.

If Cupitt and Norman are taken seriously, then we must acknowledge that the crisis of renewal has now been overtaken by a crisis in renewal itself. Surely many anxious observers, hoping for a word of hope and assurance in the midst of the turmoil and confusion of the contemporary church, are by now at their wits' end. The task of fixing the church, they may say, has simply made matters worse by driving its advocates to the kind of polarized extremes on display in Cupitt and Norman. We can think of two responses to this impasse. We can imagine one group thinking that it is time to get off this train and begin all over again in earnest. It is time, they say, to cut our losses, to abandon the church, and to start afresh in the Holy Spirit. We can imagine another group thinking that we need to stand back and face the awkward truth that there are no prospects for effective renewal. It is time, they say, to stop harping on our utopian theological aspirations and settle in for a long and unpleasant sojourn in the ecclesiastical sewer. We must face these options head on if we are to make progress in the renewal of the church.

CHAPTER 8

QUAKING IN THE RUINS

C. PETER WAGNER AND R. R. RENO

WE HAVE ENCOUNTERED IN OUR JOURNEY thus far what we might accurately depict as the doorknob theory of renewal. The theory runs like this: In entering the church, a bright and alert member notices that the doorknob needs polishing. In time others join him, but they then notice that the door itself is in need of painting. So another enterprising member sets out to paint the door, and a hardworking crew soon joins her. On the way in through the newly painted door, a third member notices that the vestibule is terribly cluttered and untidy, and he sets about clearing it up in earnest. He is keen that newcomers do not get the wrong impression on their first visit. Other members do not like the music and insist on updating the tempo and the lyrics. In reaction to this move others threaten to leave and set about strengthening the traditional forms of worship with gusto. By now fixing the building has become something of an obsession for many of the members.

In time the architects show up and begin looking at the foundations. They claim to be trained experts and specialists. Unfortunately they do not agree on either the structure or the original layout of the building, nor on its developments over the years at the hands of later occupants. Worse still, they have radically different plans drawn up for either restoring the building to its original beauty, or for renovating it in a fitting way to meet current expectation and needs. Not surprisingly, by this time the noise in the church has become cacophonous, and the building begins to fall apart, as rival teams of workers assault it. In the meantime, many members have been sneaking out to look at other buildings in the neighborhood that seem to have exciting new architects. So some of them leave to join these new architects and to start all over again. Others make their way down into the basement and settle in to endure the chaos above.

The impulse to exit is represented by an enterprising entrepreneur from the heart of the evangelical establishment in Fuller Theological Seminary; the second by a dashing young theologian from within the heart of the mainline establishment at Yale Divinity School. In this chapter we want to explore the response to renewal represented by C. Peter Wagner (1930-) and R. R. Reno (1959-). The former is a renowned expert in church growth, who now works freelance, and who has given extensive attention of late to developments in Pentecostalism. The latter is an American Anglican, who has a distinguished track record as a student of widely influential Yale theologian George Lindbeck, and who currently teaches among the Jesuits at Creighton University.

Wagner's convictions about the current situation in the church and its future direction are derived from his empirical observations. He has studied churches of all sizes, in diverse locations, spanning the gamut of theological tradition, and rooted in six different cultures across six continents. In his first season of research, from 1970 until the 1980s, he spent his time researching the technicalities of church growth. Reluctantly and gradually he began to notice that the churches that grew most rapidly were those that "outwardly featured the immediate present-day supernatural ministry of the Holy Spirit."[1] Under the inspiration of John Wimber, he then turned to a season of research in which he focused on the spiritual principles of church growth. Thus he attended to the relationship between supernatural signs and wonders and church growth, and then to the place of prayer and spiritual warfare in church growth. This took him from the early 1980s through the mid-1990s. It is within his third period of research, from the mid-1990s to the present, that we find the material of interest to us here. The churches that he has come to

---

1. C. Peter Wagner, "The New Apostolic Reformation," in C. Peter Wagner, ed., *The New Apostolic Churches* (Ventura, Calif.: Regal, 1998), p. 14. Wagner lays out his views more fully in Wagner, *Churchquake* (Ventura, Calif.: Regal, 1999).

call "new apostolic churches" operate in such a way as to combine both technical and spiritual principles of church growth. It is these churches that are pivotal for the future of the church as a whole. They provide the new forms or wineskins for the church of the future.

The existence of these new developments signals the end of renewal efforts in traditional forms of Christianity. Wagner leaves no room for doubt:

> Especially since the 1960s, denominational "renewal movements" have proliferated in almost every traditional denomination. They have sensed a call of God to remain in their denominations in order to pray for and work for renewal. None that I have been aware of have been successful. The denominational leaders, true to their ideal of pluralism, have tolerated them, but the problems of control, power, and particularly management of financial resources have caused them to domesticate the renewal movements, a skill at which they are competent. What renewal might have taken place is largely cosmetic.[2]

There is nothing in empirical observation per se to suggest that these shifts in the research interests of a contemporary church growth theorist represent the unfolding of God's plans for the church over the centuries. For that we need a theological narrative of church history. Happily, Wagner supplies both a formula and a narrative that can help us at this stage.

As Wagner sees it, the letter to the Ephesians supplies the blueprint for church growth.[3] Formally, Wagner is a traditionalist at this point, seeking to derive his vision of the church from the New Testament.[4] Ma-

---

2. Wagner, *Churchquake*, p. 149.

3. Wagner takes his cues from Ephesians 4.

4. Elmer L. Towns in his Foreword to the essays assembled by Wagner insists that "these new churches are not changing the essentials of Bible doctrine. They are as committed to the fundamentals of the faith as the originators of past conservative denominations were committed to the essentials of Christianity. They are merely changing the methods of evangelism, worship, Bible study and leadership." See Wagner, *Churchquake*, p. 9. Wagner describes himself as "a very traditional Christian. For decades I have been a congregational minister, and I still am. . . . Furthermore I am a conservative Congregationalist (ordained in the Conservative Congregational Christian Conference)." See Wagner, *Churchquake*, p. 16. Elsewhere Wagner identifies the conservative bent of the new churches in this fash-

terially, we can detect the articulation of two fundamental principles. Unity (joined together) + gifts (every part does its share) = growth, is the formula. More propositionally, Christ gives gifts to his church on two levels: on the governmental level (apostles, prophets, evangelists, pastors, teachers) and on the level of the ministry of the saints in general, where each receives his or her own gifts for ministry. For two thousand years these principles have been at work in the history of the church. Jesus promised to build the church, and he has clearly done so. However, Jesus does not always build his church in the same way.

> He did it one way in the Roman Empire before Constantine; another way after Constantine; another way in the Middle Ages; another way following the Reformation; another way during the era of European colonization; and yet another way post–World War II, just to name a few.[5]

Each new way brings new wineskins. Thus the story of the church can be reconstructed as the story of new wineskins for each new era. Put differently, we might say that God has blessed different ways of being the church across the ages, so that the causal explanation of the church's persistence in time requires the interaction of unceasing divine blessing and changing wineskins. Wagner does not provide all the details of this story;[6] he only zeroes in on the most recent changes in wineskins. Thus the new wineskins of the 1970s were those supplied by Pentecostalism. By 1993 he detected a change in wineskins, as he studied the African Independent Churches, the Chinese house churches, and Latin American grassroots churches.

---

ion: "Many of the characteristics of traditional Christianity are not being changed. For one thing, the bedrock theology of the Protestant Reformation is not up for revision. New apostolic leaders are not questioning justification by faith or the priesthood of all believers or the authority of Scripture. The Apostles' Creed maintains a high profile as an acceptable summary of the doctrinal foundations of the Christian faith. New apostolic churches continue to celebrate Christmas and Easter." See Wagner, *Churchquake*, p. 18.

5. Wagner, "The New Apostolic Reformation," p. 15.

6. He endorses at one point a simple schema that divides the history of the church into three eras: "The Apostolic Paradigm" (first to third centuries), "The Christendom Paradigm" (fourth to mid-twentieth centuries), and the "New Apostolic Paradigm" (late twentieth century to twenty-first centuries). See Wagner, *Churchquake*, p. 37.

How are we to identify the new wineskins that God is now blessing? To do so we need to explore the common characteristics shared by these, the fastest-growing segments of Christianity in the world. What he finds is nothing less than a "churchquake," "the most radical change in the way of doing church since the Protestant Reformation."[7]

Wagner goes on to cite nine features of this change. First, we have a new apostolic reformation in which outreach is combined with a recognition of present-day apostolic ministries. While both of these have been accepted to some degree in traditional churches, their primary form and location are in loosely structured apostolic networks. The names of these local churches vary across the world (everything from the "Crystal Cathedral" to the "The Warm Body of Jesus" to the "Dodge the Devil and Go Straight to Heaven Church") but the substance remains the same.

Second, there is a transition from bureaucratic authority to personal authority, from legal structure to relational structure, from control to coordination, and from rational leadership to charismatic leadership. At the local level, new apostolic pastors have emerged as leaders, compared to employees in traditional Christianity. At the translocal level, the office of apostle has reemerged — that is, those sent out with a commission. We have literally the full recovery of apostles in the contemporary church.[8]

Third, complementing new patterns of leadership, there is a dedication to releasing the people of the local congregation to do the ministry of the church. Thus members are taught to identify their spiritual gifts and natural talents. From these same members staffs of local churches, who bypass the traditional methods of training, are recruited. So "new apostolic ordination is rooted in personal relationships, which verify character, and in proven ministry skills."[9] Many of these new apostolic churches are establishing their own, in-house Bible schools.

Fourth, where traditional churches start with the present situation

---

7. Wagner, "The New Apostolic Reformation," p. 19.

8. Wagner himself is now identified as, and accepts the designation of, the "Presiding Apostle for the International Coalition of Apostles." He has explored the issue of the restoration of apostles and his own call and recognition as an "apostle" in Wagner, *Spheres of Authority* (Colorado Springs: Wagner Publications, 2002).

9. Wagner, "The New Apostolic Reformation," p. 21.

and focus on the past, "new apostolic Christianity starts with the present situation and focuses on the future."[10] Thus new apostolic leaders are driven not by a heritage but by a vision.

Fifth, liturgically, new apostolic churches use contemporary worship styles:

> Worship leaders have replaced music directors. Keyboards have replaced pipe organs. Casual worship teams have replaced robed choirs. Overhead projectors have replaced hymnals. Ten to 12 minutes of congregational singing is now 30 minutes to 49 minutes or even more. Standing during worship is the rule, although a great amount of freedom for body language prevails.[11]

Sixth, new prayer forms have emerged inside and outside the church. Thus some churches practice concert prayer in which all worshippers pray out loud at the same time. "For many, prayer marches, prayer-walking, prayer journeys and prayer expeditions have become part of congregational life and ministry."[12]

Seventh, new apostolic churches experience few financial problems, for three reasons: generous giving is expected; giving is presented as beneficial to the giver, like seed producing fruit in the harvest; and giving is a cheerful occasion often marked by excitement and celebration.

Eighth, new apostolic churches are aggressively committed to outreach and to the planting of new congregations at home and abroad. Within this, "compassion for the poor, the outcast, the homeless, the disadvantaged and the handicapped is a strong characteristic of most new apostolic churches."[13]

Ninth, new apostolic churches share a new orientation to the supernatural power of the Holy Spirit. Here there is a reversal of the old order of truth and then access to power, so that supernatural power tends to open the way for applying truth. The power of the Holy Spirit is medi-

---

10. Wagner, "The New Apostolic Reformation," p. 21.
11. Wagner, "The New Apostolic Reformation," p. 23.
12. Wagner, "The New Apostolic Reformation," p. 23.
13. Wagner, "The New Apostolic Reformation," p. 24.

ated through a variety of media: "It is commonplace . . . to observe active ministries of healing, demonic deliverance, spiritual warfare, prophecy, falling in the Spirit, spiritual mapping, prophetic acts, fervent intercession and travail, and so on in new apostolic churches."[14]

Given these patterns of development, it is clear that we have a major transformation of Christianity on our hands. This is nothing less than a reinventing of world Christianity. If this is the case, it is not surprising why the old-line churches are failing. They are wedded to forms of ministry that God once blessed, but their wineskins are now obsolete, given the new work God is doing in the new apostolic churches. The way ahead is obvious. We should give thanks to God for allowing us to be alive and active in his kingdom today. In being active we have essentially three options. If we are in the old line, we can revise and update the forms of the faith by bringing them into alignment with God's current plan of blessing. If not, we can join ourselves to one of the new apostolic churches. Alternatively, we can launch forth and begin a new apostolic congregation, deploying the new wineskins that the Holy Spirit is now supplying for today.

Reno's proposals are diametrically contrary to those developed by Wagner. Wagner is so taken with the exciting developments he perceives taking place outside mainline Christianity that he seeks to dwell within the new forms he discerns emerging there. He shrinks from exposing the implied judgment that the mainline option is now obsolete and in serious trouble. Reno, on the other hand, is resolute in painting the ruin of the mainline, and he is equally resolute in resisting the move to leave and find better, greener pastures. Indeed he thinks that the push to distance ourselves from the current forms of the church is precisely the sin of virtually all forms of modern Protestantism. Both liberals and conservatives are smitten with the urge to distance themselves from the church, and to envision and create an alternative, ideal reality in which to dwell.

What makes Reno so interesting is that he is ruthless in describing the negative side of contemporary mainline Christianity. More precisely, he is ruthless in describing life within his native Anglicanism, for Reno,

14. Wagner, "The New Apostolic Reformation," p. 25.

while he thinks his own denomination is relatively typical of the state of mainline Christianity, sticks tightly to developments within his own tradition.

His primary image for describing the current state of the church is that of ruins:

> As a believer in the now late (or post) modern West, I suffer the diminishment and debilitation of Christianity. The church . . . is in ruins. If you, the reader, have faith, then you suffer this ruination as well. It is the great and inescapable fact about modern Christianity. To be in the church is to endure a broken form of life. . . . However winsome might be individual stones, the walls of the church have been thrown down and the gates of its sanctuaries are broken. If you will but open your eyes, you cannot help but see the ruins. . . . We must bear the reality of the church and wear the fetters that our age has given us to wear: an increasingly inarticulate theological tradition, a capitulating and culturally captive church, a disintegrating spiritual discipline.[15]

Clearly, on this analysis, the church is in serious trouble. She is saddled with compromises, with a smug and increasingly irrelevant establishment, with faithless leadership, and most of all with fragmentation and division. Not surprisingly, the temptation to put distance between ourselves and the church is endemic. The great modern project from Descartes onward has been to separate ourselves from the reality of the church and to sweep away whatever we find uncongenial. By separating we are promised a purifying preparation of our souls that enables us to rebuild and reconstruct without the burden of a disordered and failed inheritance. The Irish Anglican, John Nelson Darby, who set up his own pure church, only to leave it when it turned out to be flawed as well, developed the most radical ecclesiastical version of this strategy in the nineteenth century. His legacy lives on in the dispensationalism canonized

---

15. R. R. Reno, *In the Ruins of the Church: Sustaining Faith in an Age of Diminished Christianity* (Grand Rapids: Brazos Press, 2002), pp. 14-15.

and widely used in evangelical and Fundamentalist circles in the Schofield Bible. The same strategy of distancing is at work in those contemporary revisionist theologians who see a church ruined by traditions of patriarchy, homophobia, exclusion, and repression, and set out to demolish it from within and make way for new structures.

Reno himself adopted for a time a somewhat less stringent version of the same strategy for dealing with the ruined state of the church:

> As an appreciative reader of Karl Barth, I thought that I had a place to stand, a place of articulate and sophisticated scriptural vision from which to correct errors and speak truths. As an Episcopalian with Anglo-Catholic leanings, I felt the liturgical life of the church to be a stable rock amidst the admittedly troubled ecclesiastical waters. So, for reasons that often make Anglicans seem hopelessly conceited, I imagined myself standing against the spirit of the age, drawing on the clarity of the Protestant confessional tradition and the stability of the Catholic sacramental system. Here I could stand at an appropriately critical yet faithful distance from the failures of Christian witness in the modern age.[16]

He was driven from this safe haven by the work of another Episcopalian, Ephraim Radner, whose book, *The End of the Church*,[17] showed him that the problem was much deeper. Radner convinced him that the tribulations of modernity are not external to the church, that modernity is nothing less than "a cultural extrusion of the hot magna of ecclesiastical affairs."[18] There was now an infection inside the body that could not be cured by a theological redeployment of the tradition or a punctilious sacramental piety. This strategy, like its more robust cousin of aggressive distancing, was a refusal to suffer the failure of apostolic witness to bind us together in love. Turning to doctrinal purity, apostolic succession, *sola*

---

16. Reno, *In the Ruins*, p. 23.

17. Ephraim Radner, *The End of the Church: A Pneumatology of Christian Divisions in the West* (Grand Rapids: Eerdmans, 1998). Reno describes wittily his own work as Radner without tears. Radner's style is exceptionally dense and even obtuse.

18. Reno, *In the Ruins*, p. 23.

scriptura, Petrine primacy, the Great Tradition — all these are strategies to turn away from the particularity of the forms of the apostolic witness when we encounter spiritual impotence and weakness in the church. They are ways of making distance and separation a form of faithfulness.

Reno's reading of modernity and its refusal of Christianity is an interesting one. Initially, modernity took the form of a confident humanism that was full of hope for the future. This humanism was redemptive. Its patron saints were Ralph Waldo Emerson, with his unbounded enthusiasm and hot passion, on the one side, and John Locke, with his sweet reason and more cautious disposition, on the other. The central driving forces were a zeal for freedom and a cool empiricism. Modern Christian theologians attempted to co-opt these trends, riding the tiger of humanism in their efforts to evangelize Western culture.

This culture, and the theology of mediation that served it, are now in disarray: "The Agent Orange of cultural critique has deforested our cultural imaginations, and we no longer imagine ourselves to be heralds of freedom and truth."[19] Ambition and confidence has been displaced by fear and anxiety. The potencies and powers that give human life its dynamism are now laden with danger. What was hailed as a breakthrough to dignity, freedom, and progress is now seen as full of menace:

> Individuality remains a cherished ideal, but the multicultural agenda places that ideal in the quicksand of race, class, and gender. For all our humanistic faith, we are not great believers in the intrinsic goodness and integrity of human nature. We shrink from the harsh disciplines that might shape our souls, even the humanistic disciplines of authenticity and rational inquiry. We need years of therapy in order to overcome our self-doubt, and even then any subsequent self-trust is fragile. Still further, we worry about ideology and wring our hands over the inevitable cultural limitations that undermine our quest for knowledge. The bogeyman of patriarchy is everywhere; everything depends on one's perspective. In all this the effort is not Emersonian ambition or Lockean confidence in reason. Pronouns are changed,

19. Reno, *In the Ruins,* p. 35.

symbols are manipulated, critiques are undertaken, but most always in the spirit of a new conformity that fears imprisonment without cherishing freedom, flees from error without pursuing truth.[20]

We can see the full force of this shift in the truisms of postmodernity: "Language is a vessel of power that seeks domination. Truth claims are tinged with imperial ambition. Technology alienates us from life. Economic dynamism produces rapacious inequality."[21]

In these circumstances the challenge to Christian evangelism is daunting indeed. Postmodern culture seeks to serve humanity by saving it from any and all power and by protecting us from the demands that lead to change. All authoritative claims are read as acts of violence. In order to avoid any kind of submission, the authority of truth itself is denied. Everything is kept at a distance by the deployment of irony. Even the positive insights of postmodern philosophy have to be taken lightheartedly and playfully. Given these developments, any effort to reach this culture with the gospel is faced with a defensive wall that effectively neuters all power and potency. Thus the strategy of moderation or mediation, in which we seek to co-opt the themes or ideals of the culture and rework them in a Christian direction, no longer works. The strategy of distance to preserve freedom has reached a limit that cannot be penetrated by anything. The old world of pride has been displaced by a new world of sloth and cowardice that is deadly in its spiritual effects. Postmodern culture "promises freedom from the disturbances of expectations and demands. For this reason the gospel of redemption will be an offense, no matter how carefully modulated, no matter how cleverly dressed up in the finery of freedom and rational responsibility."[22]

The situation is doubly bleak because the well-meaning efforts to co-opt the themes of the earlier confident humanism have crippled the church within. Seduced by the thesis that the problems the church faced in modern culture were intellectual rather than spiritual, the church embarked on a strategy of compromise. Thus we worried "about the rela-

20. Reno, *In the Ruins,* p. 36.
21. Reno, *In the Ruins,* p. 36.
22. Reno, *In the Ruins,* p. 44.

tion between science and religion, reason and revelation, faith and understanding, assuming that the wound of modernity is primarily a matter of what counts as reasonable."[23] The real problem, however, was not one of intellect but of will, not one of thought but of obedience. Kierkegaard pointed us in the right direction here:

> People try to persuade us that objections against Christianity spring from doubt. The objections against Christianity spring from subordination, the dislike of obedience, rebellion against all authority. As a result, people have hitherto been beating the air in their struggle against objections, because they have fought intellectually with doubt instead of fighting morally with rebellion.[24]

Our real problem is horror of dependence and fear of having to change our ways and become different people. Rather than face these issues, modern theology has sought compromise and relevance. Rather than come to terms with the strategies of distance that have now reached their limit in postmodernity, the church's theologians and leaders themselves embraced a strategy of distance. So much so, the church's precious resources are now in ruins.

There is no quick fix for this predicament. Thus the return to Radical Orthodoxy championed by John Milbank and others is one more effort to find an intellectual and theoretical way forward. The retrieval of a theory of neo-platonic participation veers away in the end from the particulars of the church's life. It is one more strategy of idealization and distance. Given the jettisoning of the tradition in the modern period, "orthodox theological practice becomes an invention, a determined culling from the past, an act of imaginative recovery."[25] Radical Orthodoxy is really an effort to find inspirational reminders in the monuments of past glories of the Christian intellectual, aesthetic, and political culture. It shies away in the end from the particularities of enduring practices. Thus, "Intellectual virtuosity eclipses ecclesial obedience as the key to re-

---

23. Reno, *In the Ruins*, p. 51.
24. Quoted in Reno, *In the Ruins*, p. 53.
25. Reno, *In the Ruins*, p. 76.

newal. Theology becomes creative and inventive rather than receptive and reiterative."

There are echoes here of Edward Norman, yet Reno has his own way of charting a course for the future. It begins with a resolute acceptance of our current predicament in the ruins of the church. The first task is not to imagine, or to invent, but to come to terms with where we are and what we have received. Against the temptation to theorize,

> . . . we must keep our noses close to the ill-smelling disaster of modern Christianity, articulate about its failures, but training ourselves to dwell in enduring forms of apostolic language and practice. Diminished vision may be the price we must pay. We may not be able to see our culture, stern to stern, through Christian eyes. We may no longer be able to see the complex shape of our contemporary churches as creatures of the gospel. We can only see what has been given to us to see. But paying this price is necessary if we are to train our eyes to see the identity of Christ in the witness of scripture and the practice of the church. For no matter how we might soar on the eagles' wings of theological ideality, and despite our hopes that from such heights we might discover a vision of the full scope of the truth of Christ, we will be disappointed. Christ is the concrete faith and practice of the church, and only he can give power and potency to a postmodern theology that is genuinely orthodox. The Son holds all things together in the Father.[26]

But how are we given access to Christ at this point? Here Reno faces a difficult dilemma. On the one hand, he insists that Christ is mediated in the particular forms of apostolic language and practice. We must return to the first-order realities of the church in her scriptures, creeds, sacraments, prayers, and the like. We must dwell in the sheer givenness of the apostolic tradition, returning to the church's most primitive and basic gifts. On the other hand, these forms are deeply contaminated and compromised in the traditions through which they are mediated in, say, con-

---

26. Reno, *In the Ruins*, p. 79.

temporary Anglicanism. Thus Scripture is interpreted in a welter of historical-critical readings and becomes a cause for division, not unity. So we turn away from Scripture to spirituality, or to crisis management, or to philosophical reflection, as a way to move ahead. Equally, the Nicene Creed is seen as a linguistic artifact divorced from a living tradition of theological exegesis and hence powerless to make a difference. The historic episcopate, supposedly the guardian of the faith and the sign of unity, has itself become a hotbed of innovation and a sign of warring theological factions. The sacraments of baptism and Eucharist, now left to carry the full force of the faith, are dulled and obscured by changes in practice and hence cannot carry the weight allotted to them. It is surely a challenge of enormous magnitude to see how we can dwell in the mutilated or corrupted forms of the tradition now operating in the ruins of the church and at the same time gain access to the spiritual and theological resources that are essential to renewal. Or at least, that it is how it strikes one initially.

Reno is well aware of this and his solution is refreshingly simple. We must go back to school as best we can:

> . . . if we will dwell in the church, we will be like children who are untutored and inarticulate, who are given what they need even as they can neither understand nor contribute. We can rebel against this spiritual weakness. But if we are willing to accept the painfully unsophisticated tasks of spiritual childhood — to memorize the catechism as we once memorized multiplication tables, to hear with rapturous joy the literal sense of Scripture as we once listened to stories at nighttime, to repeat again and again the ancient liturgies as we once repeated our favorite TV shows, word for word — then we find our way forward to a theological vocation proper to those who live in the ruins of the church.[27]

This strategy of retrieving and implementing the practices of the faith will not be easy. Negatively, it means understanding and resisting the drive towards change. Thus Anglicans must overcome the desire to strike

27. Reno, *In the Ruins*, p. 96.

an affirmative pose, to distrust the particular, and to assume that change is good and inevitable. They must submit themselves to the narrowness of a law of common prayer and common life. Equally, they must resist the siren calls for sexual freedom gently but unambiguously reiterated by the Bourgeois Bohemians in their midst. This means embracing and preaching the harsh chastity of St. Paul, not because sex is the most important dimension of the Christian life, but because sexual freedom is the most cherished and most morally sanctified freedom of postmodern morality. Moreover, they must resist the superficiality of much contemporary spirituality and resubmit themselves to the actual forms of Scripture, liturgy, doctrine, and ecclesial structures given in the tradition: "we should submit ourselves to the stumbling blocks and impossibilities, these ruined walls of the church, for even in their weakened form they are integral parts of the 'rule and discipline' delivered by Jesus Christ to the apostles."[28] Through these, as through the Daily Office of Prayer, the Holy Spirit works to shape and transform. Thus the Christian life is not solitary, for the Holy Spirit "does not work upon us by inward and private means. The Church is the indispensable source and locus of discipleship. Custodian of the apostolic witness, the church draws us into the way of Jesus."[29] Contemporary scholarship may, of course, engage in endless debate about Jesus and his setting in the ancient world, but contemporary believers have in fact a clear view of Jesus:

> Good Friday and Easter Sunday are strange and alien because of the clarity of events. He may throw our lives into utter turmoil, but this man from Nazareth, who died on the cross on Golgotha and rose from a tomb outside of Jerusalem, is quite vivid. The fleshly weight of his humanity and the sharp outlines of events that have defined his life and death give Jesus Christ purchase in our souls.[30]

As we submit ourselves to the particularities and concrete of church life, the Holy Spirit forms Christ in us. Indeed, "if we are to speak of the mis-

28. Reno, *In the Ruins*, p. 145.
29. Reno, *In the Ruins*, p. 159.
30. Reno, *In the Ruins*, p. 164.

sion of the Holy Spirit, then we must make Christ the Alpha and the Omega. We must dwell more deeply in his way. There is no other mission of the Christian in the world."[31]

We are now in a position to sum up the alternatives furnished in the material supplied by Wagner and Reno. According to Wagner, we are in the midst of a new work of God. Our current problems in the church stem from our commitment to forms of church life that were once appropriate but are now obsolete. The way ahead is to reach forward into the new dispensation of the church currently being worked out in the post-Pentecostal world. Hence the mood is upbeat and radically optimistic. On the other hand, Reno sees us in the midst of the downfall of the church, brought about from within by strategies of distancing and idealistic dreaming. Rather than reach for some grand way forward, we must come to terms with the dysfunction and catastrophe that has befallen us. Thus the mood is sober and realistic. We must learn to live among the tombs, returning to a spiritual childhood of narrowness and obedience in which we dwell as best we can in the most basic and primitive forms of apostolic tradition available to us where we are.

In these two proposals we have reached the end of the line. One invites us to a transformation of the church modeled on a new work of God in the fastest-growing segment of Christianity. In this scheme the church has been effectively left behind, and we are invited to start all over again. The other summons us to survive as best we can within the ruins of the modern church. The church is dysfunctional, and we must simply live with its dysfunction. In both cases the possibility of renewal has been abandoned.

Technically speaking, Wagner does not rule out the possibility of renewal, but his heart is clearly not in this project. Nor is it likely that the mainline tradition will be persuaded by his vision. For one thing, we have seen this option before. Despite the excitement and the upbeat rhetoric, he has given us one more version of congregationalism, decked out this time in a quasi-dispensationalist theology of history driven by superficial sociological observations. The appeal to Scripture is of a piece with this.

31. Reno, *In the Ruins*, p. 164.

The biblical citations operate as a thin veneer of conservative apologetic that function merely to provide assurance in those quarters still looking to Scripture for a blueprint for the church. The new wineskins turn out to be a loose assemblage of convictions and practices that have no coherence or stability. Moreover, Wagner's romanticizing of the churches he describes ignores the harsh realities of financial mismanagement, dictatorial leadership, doctrinal aberration, egocentric triumphalism, and anti-intellectual nonsense that are also clearly visible to any candid observer.

On Reno's analysis Wagner's exuberant proposals are simply one more instance of the distancing and revision that have been the cause of the church's ruination in the West. More importantly, Reno is likely to challenge Wagner's conviction that we see in these dynamic churches the work of the Holy Spirit. We are more likely to have entirely human spirits masquerading as divine, for the church as constituted in history is the indispensable source and locus of discipleship.

We must not push the evidence further than it allows at this juncture, but there is a clear difference of orientation as regards the work of the Holy Spirit. Wagner looks over the wall of the current churches in search of the new forms that now operate as the media for the work of the Spirit. The old wineskins can no longer contain the new wine of the Spirit. Reno looks back to the roots and origins of the church and to the forms of the apostolic tradition handed over through history. To him the supposedly new apostolic forms are bogus and ephemeral.

Moreover, there is no agreement on the referent of the apostolic tradition. For Wagner, the apostolic tradition takes the form of general principles that are played out in radically different ways across the history of the church. Our task is to find and deploy the divinely given forms that fit our new situation. For Reno, the tradition is Christ himself, who is mediated by the work of the Holy Spirit through very concrete practices and materials like Scripture, creed, sacrament, and episcopal structures. To lose or damage these media is disastrous for the life of the church. She will become dysfunctional and ineffective. Rather than look around for new forms, we have to acknowledge the ruination of the church, settle in for a painful journey, and retrieve the basics of apostolic practice as best we can.

In making these judgments, Reno underestimates the level of sophistication he brings to the table. While eschewing the drive to invent new theory, and shutting off the option of escaping into some idealized vision of the faith, he cannot but deploy his own normative vision of the apostolic faith. The terse compression of the faith as represented by apostolic convictions and practices and mediated in the concrete realities of Scripture, creed, sacrament, and the like, is in itself a hard-won theological judgment. It is not some a priori discovery, nor is it an arbitrary invention. It is the distillation of a whole tradition of scholarly work that has reached a climax in recent years at Yale.

At the same time, Reno underestimates the level of sophistication needed for survival in the ruins of the church. It is fine to be reminded that we must bear the cross, suffer divine things, look for the power of God in the midst of weakness, and the like. But surely it will take vast reserves of stamina and reserves to survive in the world he describes, precisely the kind of stamina and discernment that he has developed in long years of discipleship and study. It is hard to see how new converts will be made, or how new believers might be formed seriously in the faith, if things are as bad as he insists they are. We can see this very clearly if we alter the root metaphor deployed. Suppose we look upon the situation he describes not as that of a ruined building but as that of a hospital ward badly infected with various diseases and now administered by nurses and doctors who have become ignorant, arrogant, and incompetent. Could we so readily counsel a return to basic and fundamental practices of medicine in such circumstances? That option would appear foolhardy and dangerous. It would be sidelined and effaced at every turn.

Immediately we sense that something has gone wrong on both sides. Reno is so entrapped in the ruination of the mainline that he has lost hope for the renewal of the church. He is so committed to worries about distancing that he sees nothing but trouble in looking to anything beyond the basic practices of the faith. He has been seduced by the ideology of a nostalgic conservatism. We sense intuitively a reduction of the work of the Holy Spirit. On the other hand, Wagner is so caught up in a whirl of romantic exuberance, and so immersed in his odd dispensationalist trappings, that he is blind to the work of God in the more fixed and continuous forms of the church's life. All he retains of those forms is the Bible, reduced now to a sliver of principles that are really derived from his own ruminations on the causal nexus of church growth. He has been seduced by the ideology of evangelical revisionism. Again we sense intuitively a reduction in the work of the Holy Spirit.

So we need a fresh vision of renewal that will help us do at least two things. With Reno we must uphold the historic forms of the church's life. With Wagner we cannot close our hearts and hands to the fresh insights, new practices, and renewed gifts of God that have appeared in new configurations of Christianity in the last century. We can achieve both ends if we turn afresh to the full work of the Holy Spirit that has always been available to the church across the ages. In the next chapter I shall supply a theological framework for implementing such a vision of renewal.

CHAPTER 9

RENEWAL AND THE QUEST
FOR INTELLECTUAL INTEGRITY

READING A LOT OF LITERATURE on renewal is like reading menus without being allowed to eat. One is tempted to chew paper to relieve one's hunger. Alternatively, it is like reading books on diseases without ever being able to call on the help of a doctor; one constantly runs the risk of developing spiritual hypochondria. After a while, one can easily become overwhelmed by the complexity, diversity, and density of the material available. We have sought to keep the damage as minimal as possible by focusing on a network of diverse and fascinating proposals about renewal and by calling from time to time for some basic decisions about the direction of our journey to the Promised Land.

The time has come to take stock of the terrain we have covered and to sketch a comprehensive vision of renewal that can be realistically implemented in the years ahead. In order to keep a sense of proportion I shall begin with two platitudes about renewal as a whole.

First, it is very easy for our deliberations on renewal to take the form of whining about the terrible state of the modern church. This is understandable, but it is also self-defeating and unrealistic. It is understandable because the lament and the jeremiad are a culturally favored form of discourse in the modern church. Much of our lamenting and breast-beating is really an expression of fear and anger at the loss of our position among the cultural elites of the West. When churches and their pastors have acted as the unofficial court chaplains to the culture, then the erosion of that culture and their displacement as court chaplains bring enormous pain. Hence there is a tendency to whine and complain. This is not a very healthy response to our modern predicament.

It also displays a lack of realism about all that God has done and is doing in our lives, in the church, in history, and in creation at large. However bad the church may appear, people are still brought to Christ, the Scriptures are still widely read and studied, God is still praised, extraordinary numbers of people are still interested in the Christian way, and we are still free to worship and serve God in a host of ways. Indeed in recent years we have seen an extraordinary interest in evangelism develop throughout the church. For the first time in centuries it may yet be the case that the Western churches will own this as an essential and crucial ministry in their service of God. Moreover, nothing but good can come from churches and their leaders coming to see that there is a sharp distinction between the gospel and culture. It is surely one necessary condition of the modern church recovering its true identity in its own canonical traditions. It is also a necessary condition of the church truly serving as salt and light within modern culture. Whatever the case, we cannot gainsay the fact that Christ has come, Christ has died, Christ is risen, and Christ will come again. Anyone who shares these convictions cannot entertain any ultimate pessimism about the long-term future of the gospel and the church.

Second, if we look at the long and ragged history of the church, renewal has never been comprehensive. It has been patchy, partial, scattered, disorganized, and volatile, and it has rarely lasted more than a couple of generations. Luther was too pessimistic to claim that it never lasts more than about thirty years, but he had a point. This reminds us that the battle against evil is never over. The forms that temptations take vary in amazing ways from generation to generation and even from church to church. In the 1960s we faced in some quarters a naive commitment to a secularism that was arrogant, skeptical, anti-supernaturalist, and spiritually barren. In the present situation, we may be more likely to face a stance that is credulous, superstitious, hyper-supernaturalist, and spiritually luxurious. Meanwhile, we may have to deal, as we do in Ireland, with forms of nationalism that are hopelessly idolatrous. It is important, therefore, to be persistent in faith and to expect trouble every step of the way. There is no "big bang" that will solve all our problems; there is no spiritual hurricane that will sweep in off the coast and blow evil away; there is no spiritual vaccine that will prevent the arrival of new viruses; there is no new messianic figure waiting in the wings to lead us to earthly glory. The final renewal of creation will be apocalyptic in character. We dare not forget this in our enthusiasm to see God's future break in upon us here and now. We must embrace a persistent repentance and a sobering optimism in the face of God's final judgment and ultimate transformation of creation.

Coming to terms with the many and varied proposals for the renewal of the church is a demanding challenge. Yet we can make some generalizations and comments that are illuminating.

To begin, it is clear that every major branch of Christianity has entered a period of intense self-analysis and self-searching. The literature we have perused bears ample testimony to the search for a way forward in difficult circumstances. Within this it is clear that different groups of Christians face very different temptations and problems. Just as it has been noted that the Irish are religious and it is impossible to make them moral, and that the English are moral and it is impossible to make them religious, so different kinds of Christians sin differently. Thus at present the obvious danger for mainline Christians is that they will engage in so many rounds of reform that there will be nothing left to reform. The tradition becomes so thinned out that it collapses from within in the ebb and flow of cultural change. For Roman Catholics the current situation is one of polarized tension, with traditionalists gradually gaining the upper hand. Yet the deep trust in leadership that this requires has been wounded by sexual scandals among the clergy. For Eastern Orthodoxy, having been given a new lease on life with the fall of Communism, the challenge now is how to come to terms with their newfound freedom without lapsing back into dependence on the state and without hiding away in its wonderful ancient liturgies. Evangelicals have suddenly found themselves called back in from the wilderness because of their skill in evangelism. They now face the challenge of ministering and working in more complex positions of power and influence, yet constantly break out into squabbles about eschatology, the nature of biblical translation, and their doctrine of God. Pentecostals are clearly at long last gaining the attention they deserve. Yet they too readily fall prey to pride, to historical amnesia, and to the lure of the spectacular and the ephemeral. Happily, the ecumenical movement has drawn Christians into deep conversation and encounter over the last century; it is vital that ecumenism be kept alive, even though the instruments of ecumenism are radically changing, and we do not know what form they will take in the years ahead.

Our survey of the literature brings into focus six major areas of concern and action. I shall indicate some of my own judgments about these issues as we proceed and catch other issues in the proposals that follow. It is good to begin by registering massive agreement across a series of significant disagreements.

First, it is heartening to report that modern Christians are in agreement in their commitment to reject racism and to promote justice. As noted earlier, Martin Luther King and Oscar Romero have won the day on this. On this front, it is important to keep in place a resolute grasp of the gospel as the arrival of the kingdom of God. It is superficial to dismiss the language of the kingdom as sexist, patriarchal discourse. Like virtually all our language about God, it is analogical, drawing on our ordinary categories yet filling them with new meaning gained from God's gracious intervention in history. This hard edge is vital if Christians are to tackle the tough demands of tyranny or to take on the soft allure of consumerism and democracy. The Christian gospel reaches to the healing of the nations, and the arrival of God's kingdom is the slipstream of that healing.

Second, it is clear that renewal has exposed a very deep fault line within much of contemporary Christianity. We indeed face a third schism, in which the central difference is how far the contemporary church will sustain the agreed faith that emerged in the patristic period. The minority position represented by Ruether, Spong, and Cupitt insists that modernity and postmodernity leave no room for even the most sophisticated or generous orthodoxy. Christianity must be radically updated and revised. Those who take a contrary position, represented most fully here by Newbigin, Ratzinger, Schmemann, Norman, and Reno, are resolute in resisting this move, and they are right to do so. The minority report is inherently unstable; it has no resources for robust forms of mission; it is hopelessly parasitic in its dependency on earlier tradition; it is devious in its use of church institutions; it is incurably polemical and aggressive in tone and manner; it is arrogant in its claims to possess the agreed results of modern scholarship; and it has ended in atheism. This does not mean that there is full agreement on the orthodox side. Indeed, finding a felicitous way to articulate the contours of the tradition without falling captive to modes of thinking that undermine it is a daunting challenge. I shall take up this challenge shortly in my own idiom.

Third, it is also clear that we face deep disagreement on the place of institutions in the life of faith. Here there is fascinating consensus that unites radicals and conservatives. The default position sees institutional forms beyond local communities of Christians as at best a necessary evil and at worst as disastrous. Often this emerges in the narrative of the church that repeats the standard shibboleths about Constantine and the fall of the church in the fourth century. Thus Draper, Spong, Ruether, Bilezikian, Cupitt, and Wagner sing much the same song. Clearly, this little choir sings out of tune when they are together, but the music is bad from the outset. Institutional practices are pivotal in the life of the church. The constant appeal to abuse to knock institutions is vastly overplayed. Furthermore, institutions have been inspired and created by God. To limit God's activity to the inner life, or to works of justice, or to the production of a holy book, is simply to deploy a thin and inadequate doctrine of creation. Equally, to opt for congregationalism and limit the unifying dynamic of the gospel to local congregations that go their own way and ignore the wider unity Christ brings is to sell the faith short.

Fourth, Christians are deeply at odds on how to read the history of Western culture. It is agreed that there has been a sea change in the West over the last two centuries. Christianity has been eclipsed in public life; a network of astute and sometimes bitter critics has challenged its beliefs and ethics; and it has declined dramatically. There the agreement ends. We disagree on the causes behind these changes; we differ on how far Christian intellectuals aided and abetted these changes; and we argue in circles as to how to respond to these changes.

Fifth, Christians are unsure about what to do with the emergence of Pentecostalism as a living, volatile, worldwide form of Christianity. This is surely the biggest surprise of the twentieth century. It dramatically goes against the grain of decline in the West. To some Christians, it represents a return to an impossible form of supernaturalism, complete with dreams, visions, and exorcisms. To others, it is the one sign of hope for the future. It undermines in one fell swoop the restrictive naturalism of Western intellectuals and their theological chaplains. It restores a pivotal element in the life of Jesus and the witness of the early church. It gives fresh energy and drive for witness and service. It makes theism a lively option again. At one level, Pentecostalism confirms the conviction that some form of orthodoxy is the only way ahead. At another level, Pentecostalism scares the daylights out of traditional Christian theists.

Sixth, within the literature on renewal there is a recurring tendency to cast the issues in intellectual terms. Thus the drive to offer a diagnosis and prescription in terms of some favored theory of knowledge is very powerful. We have seen this crop up in different forms in Draper, Newbigin, Spong, Ratzinger, and Cupitt. In less pronounced forms, theories of knowledge as they relate to theology are crucial for Bilezikian, Norman, and Wagner. Clearly, the desire to come to terms with the Enlightenment plays a role here. Moreover, if theories of knowledge are pivotal, then it is obvious that philosophy must play a decisive role in renewal.

Yet this is where we must immediately pause, for surely we are not healed or saved by philosophy. We are saved and healed by the living God. So we are now at a point to begin the outline of an alternative vision of renewal. The key to the renewal of the church is the varied workings of the Holy Spirit, the Lord and Giver of Life. We can express this provocatively by saying that the church is from beginning to end a charismatic community, a community brought into existence, equipped, guided, and sustained by the Holy Spirit.

Our Lord Jesus Christ instituted the church; the Holy Spirit constituted the church. Jesus Christ himself was a gift of God the Father, given in the virgin womb of Mary, through the working of the Holy Spirit. He preached, taught, healed, and cast out demons in the power of the Spirit.

He was led into the wilderness by the Spirit, he gave up his life on the cross through a mighty act of the Spirit, and he was designated Son of God in power according to the Spirit by his resurrection from the dead. Jesus Christ, our great God and Savior, in turn promised to send the Holy Spirit to all who believed the gospel and joined themselves in faith to him. Not surprisingly, at Pentecost the church came into existence when the Spirit came upon and within the waiting disciples.

From the beginning, there were charismatic gifts in the church. These were varied, serving the diverse needs of the body and her ministries. The gifts were so abundant that no formal list was adequate to capture their nature or number.

From the beginning, there was also the fruit of the Holy Spirit, manifest in the lives of Christ's followers in love, joy, peace, patience, kindness, goodness, faithfulness, gentleness, and self-control.

Furthermore, there were a variety of charismatic experiences in the life of the church. Unbelievers were convinced of sin, of righteousness, and of judgment by the Holy Spirit. Believers and unbelievers were baptized in the Spirit; they were immersed in the power and light of the Spirit. They came to call God, "Abba, Father," through the internal witness of the Spirit; and they learned to discern the workings of the Spirit in their work and ministry.

There were also charismatic offices in the early church. Over time the community, led by the Holy Spirit, set aside individuals to serve as deacons and elders. The Spirit set aside others to work as apostles, prophets, evangelists, pastors, and teachers to equip the saints for the work of ministry. Eventually, they included bishops and overseers, superintendents and shepherds, who had the responsibility to ensure that the apostolic traditions were transmitted across the generations.

These apostolic traditions and their development were themselves inspired by the Holy Spirit. They were not merely a human response to the great salvation that had come through Christ; they were the divinely guided interpretation of God's mighty acts in incarnation, atonement, and resurrection for the liberation of the world.

The formal reception of these traditions within the church took place in charismatic events in the life of the church, that is, in conferences and councils. It is hard for us to think of church conferences and conventions as charismatic events. Our ecclesial decisions have become so politicized and secularized that cynicism is now the standing order of the day. Our division into parties, the unashamed use of caucuses, the relentless use of political rhetoric, the resort to the practices and the gimmicks of modern public relations — all these manifest a deep distrust in God and a desire to lord it over others as the Gentiles did. This is neither what councils initially were nor what they were meant to be. The early councils were charismatic moments and events in the life of the church. The leaders trusted the Holy Spirit to lead them into the truth, as Christ had promised, and they had the nerve to say, "It seemed good to the Holy Spirit and to us."[1]

The traditions inspired by the Holy Spirit were varied and served very different, complementary functions. The most important traditions were canonized, that is, listed and publicly adopted by the church as a whole. For the sake of convenience, we shall call this the canonical heritage of the church.

Chief among the inspired traditions were the books that later were added to the Hebrew Scriptures and were designated as the New Testament. The very canonical ordering of the texts was no accident. A distinction was drawn between what was old and new in the testaments of God, and a further distinction was drawn between the gospels and the other literature of the New Testament. Paul, himself no less than an apostle, called and vindicated by the working of the Holy Spirit, was given a position of secondary honor, a position which was tragically reversed at the Reformation.

Alongside the Scriptures, other canonical material was added. There were the great creeds of the church, ultimately culminating in a universally agreed-upon rule of faith known as the Nicene Creed. There was the development of appropriate liturgical canons to serve as standards of worship and praise. Sacramental acts and other liturgical drama were worked out and stylized. Various spiritual disciplines were identified. Sanctified forms of iconography were invented to capture visually the content of the gospel. Individuals who exemplified conspicuous sanctity

---

1. Acts 15:28.

were listed as saints and thus became models and inspirations of faithfulness. Certain writings and teachers were identified as possessing special insight into the nature and meaning of the faith; they were listed or canonized as Theologians and Fathers. And in order to ensure that this network of materials, practices, and persons were taken with appropriate seriousness across space and time, overseers or bishops were appointed and charged with the task of teaching, preserving, and protecting them.

To see this canonical heritage as a gift of the Holy Spirit or as the life of the Holy Spirit in the church radically alters how the various elements are received. In an informal way, the tradition itself indicated that these were not merely human productions, but unique elements in the life of faith. They had very specific purposes that needed to be constantly borne in mind as they were appropriated.

Their central purpose was to make known to God's people the mind of Christ. In his person, so fully human as to be born of a teenage virgin in Bethlehem and to be crucified ignominiously under Pontius Pilate, one encountered the very being of God. The creeds themselves made clear that all the treasures and truth of God were hidden in him in all their fullness. Nor was coming to know the mind of Christ merely an intellectual exercise. It involved gaining salvation and liberation, entering into the rule of God in the world, here and now. Such salvation was quite impossible without the working of the Holy Spirit in the depths of one's personal being, challenging hidden corners of corruption and sin. This makes possible repentance, a change of mind, and a turning to the living God in faith. As one acquired the Holy Spirit, as one was baptized in the Holy Spirit, one was drawn deeper into the life and work of Christ crucified, and this in turn took one down into the very depths of God's mysterious, transpersonal reality. From beginning to end there is comprehensive, personal transformation that restores us to our true destiny as children of God. In the midst of this there is plenty to say and hear, in tongues known and unknown. Christians talk, pray aloud, sing, and even shout. In the end, however, all our discourse trails off into silence. Immersed in the canonical heritage of the church, through the working of the Holy Spirit, we are drawn into the very being of God and lost in a speechless silence of wonder, love, and praise.

It remains only to add that the church spread through the power and working of the Holy Spirit. The early Christians gossiped the good news across the length and breadth of the Roman Empire. The Holy Spirit witnessed to the Word of the gospel internally in the hearts and minds of the hearers, and externally in signs, wonders, and feats of suffering and martyrdom. Outsiders were drawn into the fellowship of the church, a fellowship that was itself a fellowship in the Holy Spirit, and they were initiated into the rich, diverse, and informally ordered canonical traditions of the Christian heritage.

We can be grateful, then, that charismatics and their admirers have drawn attention to the critical significance of the working of the Holy Spirit in the life of the church. We cannot, however, follow them in any great detail. They have opened up a window of perception, but the window is woefully inadequate on its own. Outside the full building so generously provided by God, it will break and crack under the pressures of modernity. This has already happened in many places. Christians ill-informed about the great spread of the workings of the Holy Spirit have relied on some favored aspect of that work as a holy laborsaving device. The results are predictable. Broad swathes of tradition have been despised and rejected as merely human and dispensable. The sacraments have been ignored. The long and tumultuous history of the church has been dismissed as a hiccup in the life of God. Good, pious people have exalted their leaders as messianic figures, preparing the ground for financial and moral scandal. The kingdom's works of justice and liberation have been dismissed as alien and foreign to the interests of the church. The intellect has been despised as demonic. Groups have sprouted here and there, often indifferent to the unity of the body which the Spirit wills to bring to us. We can all draw up our own catalogue of woes.

The root cause of these ills is surely obvious. They all stem in one way or another from a displacement of the canonical heritage from its primary place in the life of the church or from a willful or unintended narrowing of the working of the Holy Spirit in the history of the church. They involve a one-sided emphasis on this or that aspect of the working of God at the expense of all that God has done and promises to do for his people. The fundamental grammar of renewal is to abandon such narrowness, acknowledge the extraordinary generosity of God, and ask for a fresh outpouring of mercy and grace on the length and breadth, the height and depth of the church.

> And I tell you, ask, and it will be given to you; seek, and you will find; knock and it will be opened to you. For every one who asks receives, and he who seeks finds, and to him who knocks, it will be opened. What father among you, if his son asks for fish, will instead of a fish give him a serpent, or if he asks for an egg, will give him a scorpion? If you then, who are evil, know how to give good gifts to your children, how much more will the heavenly Father give the Holy Spirit to those who ask him![2]

As the Holy Spirit blows afresh like the wind, and as we receive, we can be sure that we will always get more than we anticipated. We will be in error, therefore, if we try and freeze the work of the Spirit into the channels and forms with which that work was initially associated. It is better to relax and be open to the fullness, ingenuity, and complexity of the life of the Holy Spirit in the church. We must have for our treasure what is old and what is new.

Critical observers will have noticed by now that there has not been a single word thus far in this chapter about epistemology or about the Enlightenment and its aftermath. They will very naturally ask, if renewal is the work of the Spirit, how can we maintain this and equally sustain the quest for intellectual responsibility that has been such a marked feature of the modern church? Can we speak in this manner and equally profess a commitment to truth and knowledge? Can we bring this kind of discourse into the modern academy without covering our heads and lying low for a season? We surely can, provided we bear in mind the following narrative of our current theological predicament.

We can begin by recognizing that the modern obsession with epistemology began in earnest in the wake of the Reformation. René Descartes's dilemma about the foundation of knowledge was not just a mat-

---

2. Luke 11:9-13.

ter of coming to terms with the rise of natural science. It was also a very natural response to the intellectual agony precipitated by the inability of Christians to reach agreement on the identity of their ecclesial canons. Roman Catholics and Protestants were locked in battle over the relative merits of Scripture and tradition and over the grounds of theological truth claims. The genius of Descartes was to recognize that the epistemological issues raised by the Reformation could not be resolved in the terms posed by the protagonists. Indeed they required nothing less than the kind of revolution associated with the founding of a new intellectual discipline. In this case the new discipline was really a new subdiscipline within philosophy, namely epistemology. To be sure, this was not exactly new. Philosophers had been intrigued with questions about the nature of knowledge long before Descartes. Descartes, however, put the field on the map and gave it an imposing central position. His proposals are now well known. He opted for a foundationalist epistemology where the first class honors went to reason and the second to experience. This was a brilliant but flawed set of suggestions, as the subsequent discussion among rationalists and empiricists makes only too clear. Even to this day we have not solved satisfactorily the questions raised by Descartes about the norms of knowledge, the criteria of truth, the nature of probability, and the like.

The questions posed by Descartes clearly have theological implications. His work, and the work of philosophers like Benedict Spinoza, Gottfried Leibniz, John Locke, Bishop Berkeley, David Hume, Immanuel Kant, and a host or others, was sometimes as much fueled by theological anxieties as it was by merely philosophical worries. In fact, Descartes felt that the theologians would benefit enormously from his deliberations.

So too did the theologians. Over time they readily took the supposed intellectual emancipation offered to them again and again by philosophy, reworking the faith to fit the fresh help furnished. What they failed to notice, however, was that Descartes's revolution had changed the terms of the debate. More specifically, they failed to acknowledge that what began as a conflict about the canons of the church had shifted to a conflict about norms in epistemology. Consequently, one of the church's canons, her scriptures, became identified as a possible norm in epistemology, to be placed alongside other putative norms with grand names like reason and experience. The Anglicans added in tradition, that poor relation in the debate about canon, as an afterthought. The various permutations made possible by combining these options in different ways and hierarchies could be used to plot the whole history of modern theological debate about canon.[3]

We need not trace that history here to recognize that it rests on a profound confusion. Christian Scripture is not a norm in epistemology. It does not solve the kind of problems that crop up in epistemology. In the nature of the case it cannot do so, for a set of diverse religious books cannot even count as a possible answer to the queries that are central to epistemology. Moreover, to press Scripture to serve this end will lead to a deep misuse of Scripture. It cuts Scripture loose from the ecclesial and spiritual context where it functions to create in us the mind of Christ, to bring us salvation from sin, and to equip us for service in the kingdom of God. Furthermore, it will lead us to ignore the fact that Scripture was one of the many lists of items given to us by the working of the Holy Spirit. It was the first and foremost canon of the church, of course, as the great teachers of the church insisted, to be used in spiritually appropriate ways along with the other canons of the church. It was not an epistemic norm that would somehow provide a divinely sanctioned solution to epistemological anxieties. Descartes stumbled inadvertently into this, and we should be grateful for his discovery.

What is now clear in the wake of several centuries of intense and brilliant debate is that the epistemological issues raised by Descartes are still with us, as unresolved as they were in his day. To be sure, we are now aware of certain unpromising roads to follow, and we have a much clearer picture than Descartes did of the complexities of the problems. This is not something that should trouble us unduly. All sorts of philosophical issues remain unresolved, so we should not panic because this set of issues is subject to discussion and debate. Any intelligent person who has been subject to the weal and woe of philosophical training and

---

3. I have attempted to do so in William J. Abraham, *Canon and Criterion in Christian Theology* (Oxford: Clarendon, 1998).

discussion can take them in stride. In fact, one reason why a culture should support the whole enterprise of philosophy is precisely because there are perennial issues which fall outside our conventional academic disciplines and which are raised by recurring features of our experience. These matters need to be investigated systematically by any culture that is serious about the life of the mind.

This also applies to debate about the epistemology of religious belief, or more precisely, the epistemology of theology. Both the churches and our culture at large should foster extended exploration of the norms that are relevant to claims about religious knowledge. These matters are intrinsically interesting, and they will become increasingly important morally and politically in a religiously pluralistic world. Thankfully, the subject has made enormous advances in the last thirty years. The work of Basil Mitchell, Richard Swinburne, Janet Martin Soskice, Alvin Plantinga, Nicholas Wolterstorff, and William Alston, for example, has ensured a hearing for these matters that was unthinkable in the late 1950s. As yet there has been no agreement, although the serious observer will be able to discern significant gains in our comprehension of the issues. My own predilection is to follow through on the lines of inquiry brilliantly opened up by John Henry Newman in the nineteenth century. Others will prefer to follow the options opened up by figures like Søren Kierkegaard, Thomas Reid, Michael Polanyi, and Ludwig Wittgenstein. Still others will want to pursue suggestions that crop up in the work of Friedrich Schleiermacher, Karl Barth, and Charles Hartshorne. Brave souls, like the noisy and erudite English theologian John Milbank, will take their cues from anti-foundationalist figures like Nietzsche and Derrida and turn them against themselves in arguing for a retrieval of Augustine. Whatever we do, there is no closing down the questions. Epistemological issues have been around a long time, and they are here to stay.

The mistake that is commonly made, however, is to think that Christians have to agree on how to solve epistemological problems, either as a general principle or as a precondition of ecclesial renewal. The root problem again is the inability to distinguish ecclesial canons from epistemic norms. Churches that are unclear about their ecclesial canons very quickly run into a plethora of difficulties. This is one lesson we can learn from recent experience within the Southern Baptist Convention. It is a lesson we can also learn from the experience of the people of God in the patristic period. The church early on reached agreement on its ecclesial canons. It did so without either raising or resolving the epistemological questions which became so prominent in modern European philosophy. This is exactly as it should be. The early church allowed a variety of philosophical options, as we can see in the standard works on the patristic period. Leading figures like Irenaeus, Tertullian, Clement of Alexandria, Origen, the Cappadocians, Augustine, and Maximus the Confessor, to name but a few, were rarely committed to some sort of formal epistemology. Their work is full of fascinating suggestions that deserve to be read and pondered. Nowhere, however, does this sort of work become canonical in the strict sense. It is approved by the church as a list of recommended reading to be taken to the university for further study. To treat them as more important than this for the life of faith is to displace precisely those canons that the church by hard experience and by divine guidance has identified as central and indispensable.

This judgment to relativize the place of epistemology in renewal is especially pertinent to those, like Ratzinger and Norman, who think that it is impossible to make progress without authoritative teaching, backed up by a doctrine of ecclesiastical or papal infallibility. What they desire is a more robust and effective form of doctrinal episcopacy. They are rightly convinced that the church cannot survive if leaders and teachers systematically reject it or constantly undermine it from within. In the former case they get carried away by their own personal opinions; in the latter they intentionally reject the faith but hold on to their offices and ministries. Yet Ratzinger and Norman are simply mistaken to think that this executive authority to discipline and dismiss requires some sort of infallibility. What is needed is appropriate nerve and skill to discipline appropriately. We need bishops and other organs of oversight to protect the treasures of the church and, if need be, dismiss those who would destroy the faith from within. Executive authority is more than enough to make this possible. The issue is one of will and nerve.

We may still take with the utmost seriousness Roman Catholic claims to possess papal infallibility. Indeed, they can be urged with renewed vigor within the church as a whole. But we need to be clear what is at stake when we do so. Strange as it may initially appear, papal infallibility is part and parcel of the effort to keep alive a doctrine of the infallibility of the Bible within the Western tradition. We can readily see why this is the case. The doctrine of Scripture alone, conceived along the lines of a criterion of truth, cannot survive without some way of resolving the perennial problem of the proper interpretation of Scripture. Clearly a criterion that is unclear is not going to satisfy those who want to use Scripture in this fashion. If we displace Scripture with reason and experience, then we abandon the foundation of Scripture. If we add tradition, we simply render the problem of interpretation even more acute, for we now have to interpret the massive tradition of the church as much as we have to interpret Scripture. Hence, the urge to end all the debate in one way or another is very intense indeed. One simple and attractive way to do this is to designate one person to carry the necessary burden by conceiving of him in the appropriate circumstances as an epistemic mechanism to do the required job. This is exactly the role assigned to the bishop of Rome in Vatican I. Thus papal infallibility is intimately linked to the thoroughly Western and thoroughly Protestant doctrine of Scripture alone. It is in fact a radical way of salvaging the doctrine. The Pope is the grandest of Protestants. He is a creation of modern Protestantism and a solution to the epistemological problems it has generated.

We know all too well by now the toil and trouble that has been caused by the quest for infallible foundations of theology. Hence we should keep all this theorizing at bay by treating it as useful midrash that helps us deal with second-order questions of truth, justification, and knowledge. After all, the doctrine of papal infallibility was not canonized until the late nineteenth century. Even some who believed in it much preferred to leave it as an unofficial part of the tradition as a whole. Clearly, this is the best way ahead for the future of papal infallibility in that organic unity we can all hope for as a gift of the Holy Spirit in the future. The same applies to Protestant doctrines of scriptural infallibility and to all other visions of epistemology that Christian intellectuals have developed. Christians can deploy these as needed in their attempts to deal with challenges to the truth of the faith. It is simply not the case that we need agreement on these theories to do what needs to be done in this arena. Nor is it the case that we need such agreement to have a robust, organic unity of the faithful. Indeed, if we insist on this condition of success, our ecumenical efforts will fail.

As I have suggested, the renewal of the church depends crucially on the recovery of the church's canons as part of a wider immersion in the workings of the Holy Spirit. As that proceeds, there is plenty of room for fresh work in epistemology. Indeed, once we stop confusing ecclesial canons with epistemic norms, we are liberated to look carefully and systematically at the material in the canons of the church that might throw light on the epistemology of religious belief but is currently ignored or neglected. I have in mind here the kind of epistemic hints, suggestions, and admonitions that crop up in the canonical literature. What do we make epistemologically, for example, of the admonition that only the pure in heart see God? Or what do we make of the epistemological significance of the inner witness of the Holy Spirit? We can also explore at length those more conscious efforts to be found in the writings of the great teachers of the church that wrestle with questions of religious epistemology. They will take us deep into questions about the nature of divine revelation, about the value of various forms of natural theology, about the interpretation of religious experience, and the like.

As we proceed, questions will naturally arise as to whether and how philosophy is to be used in the teaching of the church. Should we follow Tertullian and Karl Barth and keep Athens strictly segregated from Jerusalem? Or should we follow Thomas Aquinas and Schubert Ogden and look for a synthesis between theology and philosophy? Or are there any alternatives to these well-worn options? These are important matters. In the last two decades they have cropped up in debates about how far we should rely on various social and political philosophies, as is manifest in the upsurge of feminist, womanist, and African American liberation theologies. In many circles, natural theology has been replaced by social philosophy or cultural analysis as the foundations of the faith.

These matters need to be pursued with diligence. Especially relevant to our concerns at this juncture is the remarkable advice of Gregory of

Palamas. Palamas charted a fascinating third course between Tertullian and Aquinas. Tertullian rejected any appeal to philosophy, while Aquinas worked out a brilliant synthesis between theology and philosophy. Bear in mind that Palamas speaks here as a theologian. He sees himself as a teacher of the faithful, one appointed by the church to feed the flock of Christ. This is how he suggests we should proceed:

> What then should be the work and the goal of those who seek the wisdom of God in the creatures? Is it not the acquisition of the truth, and the glorification of the Creator? This is clear to all. But the knowledge of the pagan philosophers has fallen away from both these aims.
>
> Is there then anything of use in this philosophy? Certainly. For just as there is much therapeutic value even in substances obtained from the flesh of serpents, and the doctors consider there is no better and more useful medicine than that derived from this source, so there is something of benefit to be had even from the profane philosophers — but somewhat as in a mixture of honey and hemlock. So it is most needful that those who wish to separate out the honey from the mixture should beware that they do not take the deadly residue by mistake. And if you were to examine the problem, you would see that all or most of the harmful heresies derive their origin from this source.[4]

In a second passage, Palamas expresses his proposal more generally:

> In the case of secular wisdom, you must first kill the serpent, in other words, overcome the pride that arises from this philosophy. How difficult this is! "The arrogance of philosophy has nothing in common with humility," as the saying goes. Having overcome it, then, you must separate and cast away the head and the tail, for these things are evil in the highest degree. By the head, I mean manifestly wrong opinions concerning things intelligible and divine and primordial;

4. Gregory Palamas, *The Triads* (New York: Paulist Press, 1983), p. 28.

and by the tail, the fabulous stories concerning created things. As to what lies in between the head and the tail, that is, discourses on nature, you must separate out useless ideas by means of the faculties of examination and inspection possessed by the soul, just as pharmacists purify the flesh of serpents with fire and water. Even if you do all this, and make good use of what has been properly set aside, how much trouble and circumspection will be required for the task.[5]

I am not suggesting here that we should adopt Palamas's proposal on how a theologian should make use of philosophy. My intention is more modest. My argument is that it is unwise to construe these sorts of decisions as canonically settled in the life of the church. Along with their rival alternatives, they constitute crucial midrash that should be bundled up in a new sub-discipline within theology, identified as the epistemology of theology, and pursued with diligence. My aim is simply to show that my fundamental thesis about the logic of renewal, far from turning its back on the issues raised by the Enlightenment, celebrates the raising of epistemological questions. It welcomes the opportunity to tackle these matters liberated from a standard confusion that has bedeviled the discussion for centuries, and it looks forward to exploring options in deep conversation with the whole history of debate.

What is even more important is that the church be set free to retrieve all that the Holy Spirit makes possible through the full canonical heritage of the church. This is not a quick fix to our current problems. Nor will this process of retrieval happen overnight or according to some fixed timetable. We are looking at long-haul, persistent, cross-generational renewal. There will be great difficulties ahead, and there will be times when renewal will face setbacks. More is at stake than the adoption of an inert, archaic tradition, so we can be sure that the advocates of the canonical heritage will make mistakes. Many will falter and fall by the wayside. Moreover, we can be very sure that opponents of the canonical heritage will not be idle. Even then, we must proceed with both a passionate prudence and a quiet optimism. As Erasmus once ruefully observed, "To re-

5. Palamas, *The Triads*, p. 29.

store great things is sometimes a harder and nobler task than to have introduced them."[6] The retrieval of our full canonical identity is not an isolated matter, nor is it an end in itself. Rather, we should see it as an act of deep thanksgiving, as we open ourselves to the full working of the Holy Spirit in history and in our own lives. Even so, come, Holy Spirit, come!

6. In a letter to Pope Leo X, 1 February 1516.